TRIVQUIZ

1001

TRIVIA QUESTIONS

WEST HAM
UNITED

FASCINATING FACTS! TRIVIA BRAINTEASERS!
WRITTEN AND ILLUSTRATED BY

Steve McGarry

DESIGNED BY JOE McGARRY

T0018555

First published by Pitch Publishing, 2022

Pitch Publishing
A2 Yeoman Gate
Yeoman Way
Worthing
Sussex
BN13 3QZ
www.pitchpublishing.co.uk
info@pitchpublishing.co.uk

ISBN: 978 1 80150 015 9

Typesetting and origination by Pitch Publishing
Printed and bound in India by Replika Press Pvt. Ltd.

1001 TRIVIA QUESTIONS: WEST HAM UNITED

Other books in this series:

1001 TRIVIA QUESTIONS: ARSENAL
1001 TRIVIA QUESTIONS: MANCHESTER CITY
1001 TRIVIA QUESTIONS: MANCHESTER UNITED
1001 TRIVIA QUESTIONS: NEWCASTLE UNITED
1001 TRIVIA QUESTIONS: TOTTENHAM HOTSPUR
1001 TRIVIA QUESTIONS: THIS DAY IN WORLD FOOTBALL

ACKNOWLEDGEMENTS

Thanks to Joe McGarry for his brilliant design work and his technical expertise. There would be no books without him!

Thanks to Debs McGarry for the research and art assistance.

Thanks to Luke McGarry for picking up the slack on the other features while we worked on this.

Thanks to all three for their patience!

Additional thanks to Tom and Andy at "Shoot! The Breeze" podcast and Rob Stokes for the additional research and scans!

ABOUT STEVE McGARRY

A former record sleeve designer, whose clients included Joy Division, Steve McGarry is one of the most prolific and widely-published cartoonists and illustrators that Britain has ever produced. In the UK alone, his national newspaper daily strips include "Badlands", which ran for a dozen years in The Sun, "The Diary of Rock & Pop" in the Daily Star, "Pop Culture" in Today and "World Soccer Diary" in The Sun.

Over his four-decade career he has regularly graced the pages of soccer magazines Match, Match of the Day and Shoot! and his comics work ranges from Romeo in the 1970s and Look-In, Tiger and Oink! in the 1980s, SI for Kids and FHM in the 1990s, through to the likes of Viz, MAD and Toxic! When The People launched his Steve McGarry's 20th Century Heroes series, they billed him as the world's top cartoonist.

His sports features have been published worldwide since 1982 and he currently has two features – "Biographic" and "Kid Town" – in newspaper syndication, with a client list that includes the New York Daily News and The Washington Post.

In recent years, he has also created story art for such movies as "Despicable Me 2", "The Minions" and "The Secret Life of Pets".

Although Manchester born and bred, Steve has been based in California since 1989. A two-term former President of the National Cartoonists Society, his honours include Illustrator of the Year awards from the NCS and the Australian Cartoonists Association, and he is a recipient of the prestigious Silver T-Square for "outstanding service to the profession of cartooning". In 2013, he was elected President of the NCS Foundation, the charitable arm of the National Cartoonists Society. He is also the founder and director of US comics festival NCSFest.

1001 QUESTIONS

WILLIAM ARTHUR BONDS MBE

BILLY BONDS MADE HIS REPUTATION AT **CHARLTON ATHLETIC** BEFORE JOINING **WEST HAM** IN 1967. HE WENT ON TO MAKE A CLUB RECORD 799 APPEARANCES IN 21 SEASONS BEFORE RETIRING AND JOINING THE COACHING STAFF IN 1988. LESS THAN TWO YEARS LATER, HE WAS APPOINTED **WEST HAM** MANAGER, A POSITION HE HELD UNTIL 1994. IN TOTAL, **BONDS** SPENT 27 YEARS AT **UPTON PARK**. IN 2013, **BONDS** WAS THE RECIPIENT OF THE INAUGURAL **WEST HAM UNITED LIFETIME ACHIEVEMENT AWARD.**

MARK NOBLE IS THE MOST RECENT PLAYER TO RACK UP 500 GAMES FOR **WEST HAM**. IDENTIFY THESE OTHER **HAMMERS** WHO MADE MORE THAN 500 APPEARANCES FOR THE CLUB:

1   **670** (1967-1985): HE WAS LATER **WEST HAM** ASSISTANT MANAGER TO HIS BROTHER-IN-LAW **HARRY REDKNAPP.**

2   **647** (1958-1974): 1964 FWA FOOTBALLER OF THE YEAR.

3   **647** (1967-1984): SERVED AS CARETAKER MANAGER TWICE IN 2003.

4   **598** (1977-1996): PLAYED FOR **ENGLAND** AT THE 1986 WORLD CUP.

5   **548** (1921-1937): WINGER WHO HIT 166 GOALS FOR **WEST HAM.**

6   **505** (1985-2002): **WEST HAM** CAPTAIN 1993 TO 1996.

7   **505** (1920-1935): **WEST HAM'S** RECORD GOALSCORER.

8   **502** (1959-1972): HE SCORED SIX GOALS IN A FIRST DIVISION GAME AGAINST **SUNDERLAND** AT **UPTON PARK** IN 1968.

"THE MOYESIAH"

DAVID MOYES LAUNCHED HIS CAREER AT **CELTIC**, WINNING A LEAGUE TITLE IN 1982 BEFORE PLAYING FOR **CAMBRIDGE UNITED, BRISTOL CITY, SHREWSBURY TOWN, DUNFERMILINE ATHLETIC** AND **HAMILTON ACADEMICAL.** HE SPENT SIX SEASONS PLAYING FOR **PRESTON NORTH END** BEFORE MOVING INTO A COACHING ROLE AT THE CLUB, EVENTUALLY WORKING HIS WAY UP TO MANAGER,

IDENTIFY THESE OTHER **WEST HAM** MANAGERS BY THE CLUBS THAT THEY PLAYED FOR:

1 CELTIC, MANCHESTER UNITED, SWINDON TOWN

2 WEST HAM UNITED, BOURNEMOUTH, BRENTFORD, SEATTLE SOUNDERS, AP LEAMINGTON, PHOENIX FIRE

3 LEYTON ORIENT, QUEENS PARK RANGERS, NEWCASTLE UNITED, WATFORD, GILLINGHAM

4 WEST HAM UNITED, MANUREWA, NEWCASTLE BLUE STAR, KELMSCOTT, CORK CITY

5 WHYTELEAFE, EPSOM & EWELL, CORINTHIAN-CASUALS, DULWICH HAMLET, YEOVIL TOWN, CRYSTAL PALACE, CHARLTON ATHLETIC, BARNET, READING

6 WEST HAM UNITED, BIRMINGHAM CITY, ASTON VILLA, CHARLTON ATHLETIC, BRIGHTON & HOVE ALBION

7 WYCOMBE WANDERERS, WEST HAM UNITED, WOLVERHAMPTON WANDERERS, STOKE CITY, MACCLESFIELD TOWN

8 BOLTON WANDERERS, SUNDERLAND, MILLWALL, TAMPA BAY ROWDIES, COVENTRY CITY, HUDDERSFIELD TOWN, PRESTON NORTH END, WEST BROMWICH ALBION, LIMERICK

9 HAJDUK SPLIT, KARLSRUHER SC, WEST HAM UNITED, EVERTON

10 NUORESE, TORRES, NAPOLI, PARMA, CHELSEA, CAGLIARI

"MAD DOG" MANNY

AUSTRIA CAPTAIN *EMANUEL POGATETZ* SPENT A HALF-SEASON WITH *THE HAMMERS* ON LOAN FROM *VFL WOLFSBURG* IN 2013. IT WASN'T HIS FIRST TASTE OF ENGLISH FOOTBALL, HAVING SPENT FIVE YEARS WITH *MIDDLESBROUGH* EARLIER IN HIS CAREER. AN AGGRESSIVE CENTRE-BACK, HIS TIME IN THE NORTH-EAST WAS MARKED BY HIS POOR DISCIPLINARY RECORD, TWO FRACTURES OF HIS CHEEKBONE AND LOTS OF BLOOD SHED FOR THE CAUSE. HE SPENT MOST OF HIS CAREER IN GERMANY, BUT ENDED HIS PLAYING DAYS BACK IN AUSTRIA WHERE HE SUBSEQUENTLY LAUNCHED A COACHING CAREER.

FROM WHICH GERMAN CLUB DID *WEST HAM* SIGN:

1 *SÉBASTIEN HALLER* -- 2019

2 *MARC KELLER* -- 1998

3 *JAVIER HERNÁNDEZ* -- 2017

4 *HÅVARD NORDTVEIT* -- 2016

5 *DEMBA BA* -- 2011

6 *SLAVEN BILIĆ* -- 1996

7 *DIETER ECKSTEIN* -- 1995

8 *GUY DEMEL* -- 2011

MOVING ON UP

AS A PLAYER, **KEVIN NOLAN** WAS A PROMOTION SPECIALIST. HE WAS STILL A TEEN WHEN HE HELPED **BOLTON WANDERERS** GAIN PROMOTION TO THE PREMIER LEAGUE IN 2001. AFTER TEN SEASONS AT THE **REEBOK STADIUM**, DURING WHICH HE BECAME CLUB CAPTAIN, HE MADE THE MOVE TO THE NORTH-EAST IN 2008 AND ALTHOUGH **NEWCASTLE UNITED** WERE RELEGATED IN HIS FIRST SEASON, HE INSPIRED THE TEAM TO BOUNCE STRAIGHT BACK INTO THE PREMIERSHIP, WINNING THE CHAMPIONSHIP PLAYER OF THE YEAR AWARD IN THE PROCESS. SIGNED TO **WEST HAM** IN 2011, HE CAPTAINED **THE HAMMERS** TO A PREMIER LEAGUE RETURN IN HIS DEBUT SEASON. FOLLOWING SPELLS AS PLAYER/ MANAGER AT **LEYTON ORIENT** AND **NOTTS COUNTY**, HE WAS NAMED FIRST TEAM COACH AT **WEST HAM** IN 2020.

NOLAN WAS **WEST HAM'S** TOP SCORER IN THE 2012-13 AND 2013-14 SEASONS. IDENTIFY THESE OTHER PLAYERS WHO TOPPED THE **WEST HAM** GOALSCORING CHARTS:

1 STRIKER WHO FINISHED AS TOP SCORER FOR FOUR CONSECUTIVE SEASONS BETWEEN 2008-09 AND 2011-12, HE MOVED ON TO **CELTIC** IN 2015.

2 SIGNED FROM **WEST BROM**, HE WAS TOP SCORER IN THREE CONSECUTIVE SEASONS, INCLUDING 1980-81 WITH 32 GOALS.

3 SCOTTISH STRIKER WHO HIT 28 GOALS IN 1985-86.

4 BAD BOY ITALIAN WHO SCORED 17 TIMES IN 1999-2000.

5 BELGIAN WINGER WHO TIED WITH **PAUL GODDARD** ON 12 GOALS IN THE 1982-83 SEASON.

THE BOY WONDERS

BY THE TIME HE WAS 16, *JOE COLE* WAS THE HOTTEST PROSPECT IN BRITISH FOOTBALL, WITH *MANCHESTER UNITED* REPORTEDLY OFFERING £10 MILLION TO ACQUIRE HIS SERVICES. HE MADE HIS FIRST-TEAM DEBUT IN JANUARY, 1999 AT THE AGE OF 17 YEARS AND 54 DAYS, COMING ON AS A SUBSTITUTE IN AN FA CUP GAME AGAINST *SWANSEA CITY*. EIGHT DAYS LATER HE MADE HIS PREMIER LEAGUE DEBUT, AWAY TO *MANCHESTER UNITED*. HE WAS ONLY 21 YEARS OLD WHEN *GLENN ROEDER* MADE HIM *WEST HAM* CAPTAIN.

IDENTIFY THESE OTHERS WHO MADE THEIR *WEST HAM* DEBUTS WHILE STILL IN THEIR TEENS.

1   WHO BECAME *WEST HAM'S* YOUNGEST-EVER PLAYER WHEN HE MADE HIS DEBUT, AT THE AGE OF 16 YEARS AND 189 DAYS, AGAINST *LUSITANS* IN A EUROPA LEAGUE GAME IN 2015? HE WENT ON TO BECOME THE CLUB'S YOUNGEST-EVER PREMIER LEAGUE PLAYER, AGED 16 YEARS AND 237 DAYS, IN A GAME AGAINST *ARSENAL*.

2   AWAY TO *MANCHESTER CITY* IN 1996, WHO BECAME -- AT THE AGE OF 17 YEARS AND 2 DAYS -- THE YOUNGEST-EVER PREMIER LEAGUE GOALKEEPER IN WHAT WOULD PROVE TO BE HIS ONE AND ONLY *WEST HAM UNITED* APPEARANCE?

3   WHICH CENTRE-BACK MADE HIS *WEST HAM* DEBUT AGED 17 YEARS AND 179 DAYS AGAINST *SHEFFIELD WEDNESDAY* IN 1996, EARNED HIS FIRST *ENGLAND* CAP AGED 19 YEARS AND 8 DAYS, AND WAS THE WORLD'S MOST EXPENSIVE DEFENDER BY THE AGE OF 22?

4   WHICH 17-YEAR-OLD MADE HIS SENIOR DEBUT ON LOAN AT *SWANSEA CITY* IN LATE 1995 AND HIS *HAMMERS* DEBUT, AGED 17 YEARS AND 224 DAYS, AGAINST *COVENTRY CITY* IN 1996?

5   WHICH STRIKER MADE HIS *WEST HAM* DEBUT, AGED 17 YEARS AND 325 DAYS, IN A 2009 PREMIER LEAGUE GAME AGAINST *WOLVES*, EMBARKING ON A CAREER THAT TOOK HIM TO *COLCHESTER UNITED* VIA CLUBS INCLUDING *WOLVES, IPSWICH TOWN, COVENTRY CITY, NEWPORT COUNTY, PLYMOUTH ARGYLE* AND MORE?

CRESCENT STARS

CAPPED 37 TIMES BY **NIGERIA**, WITH WHOM HE WAS AN AFRICA CUP OF NATIONS WINNER IN 2013, **EMMANUEL EMENIKE** PLAYED MUCH OF HIS CLUB FOOTBALL IN TURKEY, WINNING HONOURS WITH SECOND TIER SIDE **KARABÜKSPOR** AND SÜPER LIG GIANTS **FENERBAHÇE**. HE SPENT THE SECOND PART OF THE 2015-16 SEASON ON LOAN AT **WEST HAM** BEFORE LEAVING **FENERBAHÇE** FOR GREEK CHAMPIONS **OLYMPIAKOS**.

IDENTIFY THESE **HAMMERS** WHO ALSO PLAYED FOR TURKISH CLUBS:

1 **TURKEY** WINGER WHO WON LEAGUE TITLES WITH **BEŞIKTAŞ** EITHER SIDE OF A SEASON-LONG LOAN SPELL WITH **WEST HAM** IN 2016 THAT WAS MARRED BY AN INJURY THAT RULED HIM OUT FOR ALMOST THE ENTIRE DURATION.

2 **ALGERIA** WINGER SIGNED TO **WEST HAM** FROM **VALENCIA** IN 2016. A MOVE TO TURKEY THE FOLLOWING YEAR SAW HIM WIN LEAGUE AND CUP HONOURS WITH **GALATASARAY**.

3 FRENCH RIGHT-SIDED PLAYER SIGNED FROM **BORDEAUX** IN 2007, HIS FIVE YEARS WITH **WEST HAM** WERE MARRED BY INJURY AND PERIODS OF FLUCTUATING FORM, FEATURED A LOAN SPELL AT **REAL MADRID**, AND SAW **THE HAMMERS** RELEGATED AND PROMOTED BEFORE HE LEFT FOR **ELAZIĞSPOR** IN 2012.

4 PORTUGUESE FORWARD WHO WON PROMOTION IN THE FIRST OF HIS FOUR SEASONS WITH **WEST HAM**. HAVING PREVIOUSLY PLAYED FOR **BOLTON WANDERERS, HULL CITY, HIBS** AND **BARNSLEY**, HE LEFT **THE HAMMERS** FOR **AKHISAR BELEDIYESPOR** IN EARLY 2015.

5 FRENCH STRIKER WHO, HAVING JOINED **THE HAMMERS** IN EARLY 2011, INVOKED A RELEASE CLAUSE IN HIS CONTRACT WHEN THE SEASON ENDED IN RELEGATION. HE MOVED ON TO **NEWCASTLE UNITED** AND **CHELSEA** BEFORE HEADING TO TURKEY, WHERE HE WON SÜPER LIG TITLES WITH **BEŞIKTAŞ** AND **İSTANBUL BAŞAKŞEHIR** IN BETWEEN PLAYING FOR CLUBS IN CHINA.

6 **AUSTRALIA** DEFENDER WHOSE CLUBS INCLUDE **MILLWALL, BLACKBURN, WEST HAM, EVERTON** AND **GALATASARAY**.

THE BOYS OF 1964

WEST HAM WON THE FA CUP FOR THE FIRST TIME IN THE CLUB'S HISTORY IN 1964. *RON GREENWOOD'S* MEN, CAPTAINED BY 23-YEAR-OLD *BOBBY MOORE*, BEAT SECOND DIVISION *PRESTON NORTH END* 3-2. *PRESTON* LED TWICE, THROUGH *DOUG HOLDEN* AND *ALEX DAWSON* RESPECTIVELY, BUT WERE PEGGED BACK BY GOALS FROM *JOHN SISSONS* AND *GEOFF HURST*. IN THE 90TH MINUTE OF THE GAME, *RONNIE BOYCE* WAS THE HERO WHO WON THE CUP FOR *THE HAMMERS*.

WHICH CLUBS DID THE MEMBERS OF THAT 1964 TEAM JOIN NEXT?

1 *JIM STANDEN*

2 *JOHN BOND*

3 *JACK BURKETT*

4 *KEN BROWN*

5 *BOBBY MOORE*

6 *PETER BRABROOK*

7 *JOHNNY BYRNE*

8 *GEOFF HURST*

9 *JOHN SISSON*

TEAM MEMBERS *EDDIE BOVINGTON* AND *RONNIE BOYCE* RETIRED AFTER PLAYING FOR *WEST HAM*.

THE GEORDIE LAD

A GOALSCORING LOCAL HERO WITH **NEWCASTLE UNITED**, **ANDY CARROLL** WAS SOLD TO **LIVERPOOL** IN EARLY 2011 FOR £35 MILLION, A BRITISH TRANSFER RECORD AT THE TIME. 18 MONTHS LATER, HE WAS LOANED OUT TO **THE HAMMERS**, THE MOVE MADE PERMANENT A YEAR LATER IN A CLUB RECORD £15 MILLION DEAL. **CARROLL'S** NEXT SIX YEARS WITH **WEST HAM** WERE MARKED BY A CATALOGUE OF INJURIES AND HE WAS RELEASED IN 2019 AT THE END OF HIS CONTRACT -- FOLLOWING WHICH HE RETURNED TO **NEWCASTLE UNITED**.

NAME THESE **WEST HAM** ACQUISITIONS:

1 1997: £3.2 MILLION STRIKER FROM **ARSENAL**

2 2017: £10.2 MILLION WINGER FROM **HULL CITY**

3 2014: £12 MILLION FORWARD FROM **PACHUCA**

4 2015: £10.7 MILLION MIDFIELDER FROM **MARSEILLE**

5 1997: £2.5 MILLION MIDFIELDER FROM **MANCHESTER CITY**

6 1979: £565,000 GOALKEEPER FROM **QUEENS PARK RANGERS**

7 2018: £22 MILLION CENTRE-BACK FROM **TOULOUSE**

8 2016: £36 MILLION MIDFIELDER FROM **LAZIO**

9 1979: £430,000 DEFENDER FROM **DUNDEE UNITED**

10 1999: £4.2 MILLION MIDFIELDER FROM **LENS**

11 2001: £3.5 MILLION GOALKEEPER FROM **ASTON VILLA**

12 2007: £5 MILLION WINGER FROM **FULHAM**

13 2019: £24 MILLION MIDFIELDER FROM **VILLARREAL**

14 2020: £18 MILLION FORWARD FROM **HULL CITY**

THE AFRICANS

THE MOST EXPENSIVE ACQUISITION IN **WEST HAM** HISTORY, **SÉBASTIEN HALLER** WAS SIGNED IN 2019 IN A DEAL WORTH A POTENTIAL £45 MILLION. 18 MONTHS LATER, THE STRIKER WAS SOLD TO **AJAX**. ALTHOUGH BORN IN FRANCE, AND DESPITE HAVING REPRESENTED **"LES BLEUS"** AT EVERY LEVEL FROM U-16 TO U-21, HE OPTED TO PLAY HIS INTERNATIONAL FOOTBALL FOR **IVORY COAST**, THE BIRTHPLACE OF HIS MOTHER.

WHICH AFRICAN NATION HAVE THE FOLLOWING REPRESENTED?

1 PAPA BOUBA DIOP

2 VICTOR MOSES

3 MARC-VIVIEN FOÉ

4 ABDUL RAZAK

5 HÉRITA ILUNGA

6 JOHN PAINTSIL

7 SAÏD BENRAHMA

8 TITI CAMARA

9 FRÉDÉRIC KANOUTÉ

10 PEDRO OBIANG

HARRY'S FLORIN FOLLY

IN 1994, *FLORIN RĂDUCIOIU* WON A SERIE A TITLE AND THE UEFA CHAMPIONS LEAGUE WITH *AC MILAN*, AND SCORED FOUR GOALS FOR *ROMANIA* AT THE WORLD CUP. TWO YEARS LATER, HE SCORED HIS COUNTRY'S ONLY GOAL AT EURO 1996. IT WAS ENOUGH TO CONVINCE *HARRY REDKNAPP* TO BRING HIM TO *UPTON PARK* -- BUT THE STRIKER FAILED TO ADAPT TO ENGLISH FOOTBALL AND, HAVING FALLEN OUT WITH *REDKNAPP*, WAS SOON ON HIS WAY BACK TO FORMER CLUB *ESPANYOL*.

NAME THE CLUBS FROM WHICH THESE PLAYERS WERE SIGNED DURING *HARRY REDKNAPP'S* REGIME:

1 *FRÉDÉRIC KANOUTÉ*

2 *PAULO WANCHOPE*

3 *RIGOBERT SONG*

4 *IAN PEARCE*

5 *PAUL KITSON*

6 *PAOLO DI CANIO*

7 *RICHARD HALL*

8 *SCOTT MINTO*

9 *IAIN DOWIE*

10 *SHAKA HISLOP*

11 *ANDY IMPEY*

12 *CRAIG FORREST*

13 *PAULO FUTRE*

14 *IAN THOMAS-MOORE*

THE GOAL MACHINE

THE TRANSFER FEE PAID TO **WELLINGBOROUGH TOWN** IN 1920 TO ACQUIRE THE SERVICES OF **VIC WATSON** IS UNDOUBTEDLY THE BEST FIFTY QUID THAT **WEST HAM** HAVE EVER SPENT! **THE HAMMERS** WERE REWARDED WITH 326 GOALS, A RECORD THAT STANDS UNBEATEN TO THIS DAY. **WATSON** HIT 13 HAT-TRICKS IN HIS 15 YEARS AT THE CLUB, AND IN ONE GAME AGAINST **LEEDS UNITED** IN EARLY 2019, HE BAGGED SIX GOALS IN AN 8-2 VICTORY. THE FOLLOWING SEASON, THE **ENGLAND** INTERNATIONAL HIT 50 GOALS IN 44 GAMES!

WHICH **HAMMERS** RACKED UP THESE FIRST CLASS GOAL TALLIES?

1 **252 GOALS** (1959-1972) -- SCORED 24 GOALS FOR **ENGLAND.**

2 **166 GOALS** (1953-1962) -- FIRST **WEST HAM** PLAYER TO PLAY FOR **SCOTLAND.**

3 **166 GOALS** (1921-1937) -- LEFT-WINGER WHO PLAYED IN THE 1923 FA CUP FINAL.

4 **146 GOALS** (1983-1988 AND 1994-1996) -- WENT ON TO WIN THE LEAGUE CUP WITH **LEICESTER CITY** IN 2000.

5 **107 GOALS** (1961-1967) -- STRIKER WHO WON THE FA CUP IN 1964.

6 **104 GOALS** (1970-1974 AND 1976-1979) -- **NEWCASTLE UNITED** FAVOURITE WHO HAD THREE SPELLS WITH **SUNDERLAND.**

7 **102 GOALS** (1967-1984) -- WON 47 **ENGLAND** CAPS.

8 **100 GOALS** (1953-1963) -- LEFT-WINGER WHO WON A SECOND DIVISION TITLE WITH **THE HAMMERS** IN 1958.

9 **100 GOALS** (1962-1970) -- WON THE EUROPEAN CUP-WINNERS' CUP WITH **WEST HAM** AND THE UEFA CUP WITH **SPURS.**

10 **97 GOALS** (1977-1982) -- STRIKER WHO WON THE 1980 FA CUP WITH **WEST HAM.**

IT'S A FAMILY AFFAIR

FRANK LAMPARD JOINED THE **WEST HAM** YOUTH TEAM AS AN APPRENTICE IN 1994. HIS DAD, **FRANK LAMPARD, SR.,** WAS THE CLUB'S ASSISTANT COACH AT THE TIME -- HAVING MADE 660 APPEARANCES FOR THE HAMMERS AS A **WEST HAM** PLAYER, IN A CAREER THAT SAW HIM WIN TWO FA CUPS AND EARN TWO **ENGLAND** CAPS -- AND HIS UNCLE, **HARRY REDKNAPP,** WAS THE MANAGER. THE YOUNGER **LAMPARD** SPENT SIX SEASONS IN THE **WEST HAM** FIRST TEAM, LEAVING FOR **CHELSEA** IN 2011 AFTER **REDKNAPP** AND HIS DAD WERE DISMISSED BY THE CLUB.

IDENTIFY THESE RELATIVES WITH LINKS TO **WEST HAM**:

1 TWO BROTHERS WHO PLAYED FOR **WEST HAM,** ONE LEAVING FOR **LEEDS UNITED** IN 2000, THE OTHER JOINING **SUNDERLAND** IN 2008, AND THEIR UNCLE, AN **ENGLAND** INTERNATIONAL STRIKER WHO PLAYED FOR **THE HAMMERS** IN 2003.

2 **ARSENAL** AND **BARCELONA** DEFENDER AND HIS **LIVERPOOL** AND **GALATASARAY** UNCLE, BOTH OF WHOM PLAYED FOR **WEST HAM** AND **CAMEROON.**

3 STRIKER CAPPED 59 TIMES BY **NORTHERN IRELAND,** WHO HAD TWO SPELLS AT **WEST HAM** -- IN 1991 AND THEN BETWEEN 1995 AND 1998 -- AND HIS **ENGLAND** INTERNATIONAL NIECE, WINNER OF HONOURS WITH **EVERTON** AND **LIVERPOOL.**

4 **ENGLAND** AND **WEST HAM** STRIKER AND HIS TWO SONS, BOTH OF WHOM PLAYED FOR **MANCHESTER CITY** AND **NEW YORK RED BULLS.**

5 1964 FA CUP-WINNING CENTRE-HALF WHO MADE MORE THAN 400 APPEARANCES FOR **THE HAMMERS** AND HIS DEFENDER SON, WHO SPENT FIVE YEARS AT **WEST HAM** IN THE EARLY 1990S, HAVING PLAYED UNDER HIS DAD'S MANAGERSHIP AT **NORWICH CITY.**

6 AMERICAN-BORN DEFENDER WHO MADE MORE THAN 500 APPEARANCES FOR **THE HAMMERS** BETWEEN 1984 AND 2001, AND HIS SON, WHO LAUNCHED HIS CAREER AT **WEST HAM** BEFORE FINDING SUCCESS WITH **LUTON TOWN.**

7   MIDFIELDER *ROB*, WHO MADE HIS NAME AT *CHARLTON ATHLETIC* AND *NEWCASTLE UNITED* BEFORE JOINING *THE HAMMERS* IN 2003, AND HIS SONS, *OLLY* AND *ELLIOT*, BOTH OF WHOM LAUNCHED THEIR CAREERS AT *WEST HAM*.

8   *LES, DENNIS, CLIVE, PAUL, MARTIN, OLIVER* AND CHARLIE -- THREE GENERATIONS OF PROFESSIONAL FOOTBALLERS, A NUMBER OF WHOM HAVE LINKS TO *WEST HAM*.

A KNIGHT'S TALE

TREVOR BROOKING CAME THROUGH THE YOUTH SET-UP AT **WEST HAM** -- HAVING TURNED DOWN **SPURS** AND **CHELSEA** -- AND MADE HIS SENIOR DEBUT IN 1967. IN LATE 1969, HE CHIPPED A BONE IN HIS ANKLE AND HIS RECOVERY TOOK SO LONG THAT THE CLUB SIGNED **PETER EUSTACE**. AGED JUST 21 YEARS OLD, **BROOKING** CONSIDERED GIVING UP THE GAME! HE PERSEVERED AND WENT ON TO BECOME ONE OF THE GREATEST PLAYERS IN **HAMMERS** HISTORY. HE WAS KNIGHTED IN 2004, AND FIVE YEARS LATER A STAND AT THE OLD **UPTON PARK** GROUND WAS NAMED IN HIS HONOUR. THE STANDS AT EITHER END OF THE **LONDON STADIUM** -- **WEST HAM'S** FOOTBALLING HOME SINCE 2016 -- ARE NAMED FOR **BROOKING** AND HIS FELLOW CLUB STALWART **BILLY BONDS**.

BROOKING WAS VOTED **HAMMER OF THE YEAR** A RECORD FIVE TIMES, INCLUDING THREE YEARS IN A ROW BETWEEN 1976 AND 1978. IDENTIFY THESE OTHER WINNERS OF THE AWARD:

1 *1990, 1992, 1996, 1997* -- PLAYED FOR **LIVERPOOL** IN BETWEEN TWO SPELLS WITH **THE HAMMERS**, APPOINTED MANAGER OF THE **WEST HAM WOMEN'S** TEAM IN 2014.

2 *1962* -- **SCOTLAND** INTERNATIONAL GOALKEEPER WHO LATER PLAYED FOR **STOKE CITY, MILLWALL** AND **SOUTHEND UNITED**.

3 *2013* -- **NEW ZEALAND** INTERNATIONAL DEFENDER.

4 *2002* -- FRENCH DEFENDER WHO WON THE AWARD IN HIS **WEST HAM** DEBUT SEASON, HE LATER MOVED ON TO **PORTSMOUTH**.

5 *1961, 1963, 1968, 1970* -- PLAYED 16 SEASONS AT **WEST HAM** FOLLOWED BY FOUR SEASONS WITH **FULHAM**.

6 *2009, 2010, 2011* -- WENT ON TO MANAGE **FULHAM** AND **BOURNEMOUTH**.

7 *2006* -- **WALES** DEFENDER WHO WON PROMOTIONS WITH **CARDIFF CITY** AND **CRYSTAL PALACE** AND PLAYED IN THE LOSING **WEST HAM** SIDE IN THE 2006 FA CUP FINAL.

"LIFE IS SO GOOD IN AMERICA"

PHIL WOOSNAM WAS A PHYSICS TEACHER AT LEYTON COUNTY HIGH SCHOOL FOR BOYS WHEN HE LEFT **LEYTON ORIENT** TO SIGN FOR **WEST HAM** IN 1958. HE WENT ON TO PLAY FOR **ASTON VILLA** AND EARN 17 CAPS FOR **WALES**, BEFORE HEADING STATESIDE IN 1966. HE GRADUATED FROM PLAYING FOR **ATLANTA CHIEFS** TO BECOMING COACH, BEFORE BEING NAMED MANAGER OF THE **U.S.** NATIONAL TEAM IN 1968. HE WAS COMMISSIONER OF THE **NASL** FROM 1969 TO 1982, AND LATER BECAME MANAGING DIRECTOR OF THE MARKETING ARM OF **U.S. SOCCER**, AND HELPED BRING THE 1994 WORLD CUP TO AMERICA. INDUCTED INTO THE U.S. NATIONAL SOCCER HALL OF FAME, HE DIED IN 2013 AT THE AGE OF 80.

NAME THESE **WEST HAM** PLAYERS WITH LINKS TO THE USA:

1   **BERMUDA** STRIKER WHO SUBSEQUENTLY MANAGED HIS COUNTRY'S NATIONAL TEAM, HE PLAYED 218 TIMES FOR **THE HAMMERS**, SCORING 58 GOALS, BEFORE PLAYING FOR **TAMPA BAY ROWDIES**, **TORONTO BLIZZARD** AND **PORTLAND TIMBERS**.

2   WHICH TWO **WEST HAM** MEMBERS OF **ENGLAND'S** 1966 WORLD CUP-WINNING TEAM PLAYED FOR **SEATTLE SOUNDERS?**

3   WHICH **UNITED STATES** INTERNATIONAL PLAYED FOR **MANCHESTER UNITED**, **WEST HAM** AND **BIRMINGHAM CITY** BEFORE RETURNING TO THE STATES WITH **ORLANDO CITY** IN 2017?

4   FA CUP AND EUROPEAN CUP WINNERS' CUP-WINNING GOALKEEPER WHO LEFT **THE HAMMERS** TO JOIN **DETROIT COUGARS** IN 1968.

5   NIGERIAN STRIKER WHO LEFT **WEST HAM** FOR THE STATES IN 1975. HE PLAYED EXTENSIVELY IN THE NORTH AMERICAN SOCCER LEAGUE AND THE MAJOR INDOOR SOCCER LEAGUE AND, HAVING TAKEN U.S. CITIZENSHIP, PLAYED FIVE TIMES FOR THE **UNITED STATES**.

6   HAVING PLAYED FOR **CHELSEA**, **WOLVES**, **CHARLTON ATHLETIC** AND **ASTON VILLA**, **ENGLAND** STRIKER WHO JOINED **WEST HAM** IN 2006, HE LEFT THE CLUB AFTER 11 SEASONS -- BUT RETURNED TO THE FOLD A FEW WEEKS LATER! HE WENT ON TO PLAY FOR **CELTIC** BEFORE JOINING **SACRAMENTO REPUBLIC** IN 2016.

7   WHICH **WEST HAM** PLAYER AND SUBSEQUENT MANAGER BEGAN HIS MANAGEMENT CAREER AS PLAYER-ASSISTANT MANAGER OF NASL CLUB **SEATTLE SOUNDERS** FROM 1976 TO 1979 UNDER FORMER **EVERTON** STAR **JIMMY GABRIEL?**

8   CULT FAVOURITE WHO PLAYED 284 TIMES FOR **WEST HAM** BETWEEN 1989 AND 1998 IN BETWEEN TWO SPELLS WITH **MANCHESTER CITY**. HE PLAYED IN THE STATES WITH **MIAMI FUSION** AND **NEW ORLEANS SHELL SHOCKERS** BEFORE TAKING UP U.S. RESIDENCY.

9   SCORER OF THE TWO **WEST HAM** GOALS THAT WON THE 1975 FA CUP FINAL, HE HAD TWO SPELLS WITH **VANCOUVER WHITECAPS** IN THE 1980S.

THE CZECH STOPPER

SIGNED FROM **BANÍK OSTRAVA** IN 1990, GOALKEEPER **LUDĚK MIKLOŠKO** PLAYED 56 GAMES FOR **WEST HAM** IN THE 1990-91 SEASON, INCLUDING EVERY LEAGUE GAME. HIS PERFORMANCES HELPED **THE HAMMERS** SECURE A RETURN TO THE TOP FLIGHT AND EARNED HIM THE HAMMER OF THE YEAR AWARD. HE WENT ON TO MAKE 374 APPEARANCES FOR THE TEAM BEFORE MOVING ON TO **QUEENS PARK RANGERS**. AT INTERNATIONAL LEVEL, HE WAS CAPPED 40 TIMES BY **CZECHOSLOVAKIA** AND TWICE BY THE **CZECH REPUBLIC**.

IDENTIFY THESE OTHER CZECH **WEST HAM** PLAYERS:

1 DEFENSIVE MIDFIELDER WHO JOINED **THE HAMMERS** ON LOAN FROM **SPARTAK MOSCOW** IN 2021.

2 RIGHT-BACK WHO WAS SIGNED FOR £5.4 MILLION FROM **SLAVIA PRAGUE** IN 2020.

3 DEFENSIVE MIDFIELDER VOTED 2020-21 HAMMER OF THE YEAR.

4 DEFENDER SIGNED FROM **SPARTAK MOSCOW** IN 2009, HE LEFT TO JOIN SWITZERLAND'S **BASEL** IN 2011.

5 GOALKEEPER WHO JOINED **WEST HAM** AS A TEEN IN 2006 BUT FAILED TO BREAK THROUGH, GOING ON TO PLAY FOR A NUMBER OF ENGLISH CLUBS INCLUDING **YEOVIL TOWN**, **LUTON TOWN** AND **MANSFIELD TOWN**.

6 ANOTHER CZECH KEEPER WHO FAILED TO BREAK THROUGH WITH **THE HAMMERS**, DESPITE HAVING WON LEAGUE TITLES WITH **BANIK OSTRAVA** AND **SHAKHTAR DONETSK**. HE ALSO SPENT TIME WITH **FULHAM** IN THE MID-2000S.

7 GOALKEEPER WHO HAD PLAYED FOR **NEWCASTLE UNITED**, **SHEFFIELD WEDNESDAY** AND **PORTSMOUTH** BEFORE JOINING THE HAMMERS IN 2004.

8 YELLOW CARD-COLLECTING CENTRAL DEFENDER WHO SPENT FIVE YEARS AT **WEST HAM** AFTER SIGNING FROM **FIORENTINA**.

CHAPMANIA!

LEE CHAPMAN, SON OF FORMER *LINCOLN CITY*, *PORT VALE* AND *CHESTER* STRIKER *ROY CHAPMAN*, PLAYED FOR A DOZEN BRITISH CLUBS, AS WELL AS PLAYING IN FRANCE AND NORWAY, IN A CAREER THAT SAW HIM SCORE MORE THAN 200 GOALS. POST FOOTBALL, *CHAPMAN* -- WHO MARRIED TV ACTRESS *LESLIE ASH* IN 1988 -- HAS BEEN A HIGH PROFILE RESTAURATEUR.

1 HE BEGAN HIS CAREER AT WHICH CLUB IN THE LATE '70S, PLAYING UNDER MANAGERS *ALAN DURBAN* AND *RICHIE BARKER*?

2 HE ACTUALLY MADE HIS LEAGUE DEBUT ON LOAN AT *PLYMOUTH ARGYLE* IN DECEMBER 1978 -- WHO WAS THE MANAGER, A FORMER *WEST HAM* PLAYER, WHO GAVE HIM HIS START?

3 *TERRY NEILL* SIGNED *CHAPMAN* TO WHICH CLUB IN 1982?

4 IN LATE 1983 HE JOINED *SUNDERLAND*, WHERE HE PLAYED UNDER *ALAN DURBAN* ONCE MORE. WHEN DURBAN WAS DISMISSED IN EARLY 1984, WHICH EX-*HAMMER* WAS APPOINTED CARETAKER?

5 BETWEEN 1984 AND 1988, *CHAPMAN* SCORED 79 GOALS IN 186 GAMES FOR WHICH TEAM?

6 WHO WAS THE MANAGER WHO SIGNED *CHAPMAN* TO *NOTTINGHAM FOREST* IN 1988?

7 MOVING ON TO *LEEDS UNITED* IN 1989, WHERE HE WOULD WIN PROMOTION AND A TOP FLIGHT TITLE, *CHAPMAN* WAS REUNITED WITH WHICH FORMER MANAGER?

8 A BRIEF SPELL AT *PORTSMOUTH* WAS FOLLOWED BY A 1993 MOVE TO *WEST HAM* -- WHO WAS THE MANAGER WHO SIGNED HIM?

9 HIS NEXT PORT OF CALL SAW HIM PLAY UNDER *GEORGE BURLEY* AT WHICH CLUB?

10 *CHAPMAN* ENDED HIS LEAGUE CAREER PLAYING AT WHICH SECOND DIVISION CLUB IN 1996?

34 YEARS, MAN AND BOY ...

AT 15, HE WAS A **WEST HAM** GROUNDSTAFF BOY, CLEANING BOOTS
AND PAINTING THE STANDS WHILE PLAYING FOR THE YOUTH TEAM AS
A LEFT-BACK. HE BROKE THROUGH TO THE SENIOR TEAM, ONLY TO
HAVE HIS AMBITIONS SHATTERED BY THE KNEE INJURY THAT ENDED HIS
PLAYING CAREER AT THE AGE OF 23. KEPT ON AS PART-TIME YOUTH
TEAM MANAGER, HE WORKED HIS WAY THROUGH THE RANKS AND WAS
APPOINTED MANAGER IN 1975, A JOB HE HELD FOR 15 YEARS. IN HIS
FIRST SEASON, HE WON THE FA CUP AND TOOK **THE HAMMERS** TO THE
FINAL OF THE EUROPEAN CUP WINNERS' CUP. THE SUBSEQUENT LOW OF
RELEGATION WAS TEMPERED BY THE HIGHS OF ANOTHER FA CUP FINAL
VICTORY, REACHING THE FINALS OF THE LEAGUE CUP AND A SECOND
DIVISION TITLE. AFTER 34 YEARS AT THE CLUB, HE WAS DISMISSED IN 1989
HAVING BEEN UNABLE TO SAVE THE TEAM FROM ANOTHER RELEGATION.

NAME THESE PLAYERS SIGNED TO **WEST HAM** BY **JOHN LYALL:**

1 1979: GOALKEEPER BOUGHT FROM **QUEENS PARK RANGERS** FOR
A WORLD RECORD £565,000.

2 1987: £100,00 MIDFIELDER FROM **ASCOLI.**

3 1979: SIGNED FROM **DUNDEE UNITED** FOR £430,000 MAKING HIM
THE MOST EXPENSIVE TEENAGER AT THAT TIME.

4 1976: A DOUBLE-WINNER WITH **ARSENAL,** SIGNED FOR £80,000,
A FORWARD WHO MOVED ON TO **BLACKBURN ROVERS** A YEAR
LATER AFTER FAILING TO SCORE IN 28 APPEARANCES.

5 1977: BATTERING RAM STRIKER SIGNED FROM **WEST BROM** FOR
£180,00, HE BECAME A GOAL-GETTING FAVOURITE NICKNAMED
"PSYCHO" BY THE **WEST HAM** FAITHFUL.

6 1988: HARD-MAN DEFENDER SIGNED FROM **BIRMINGHAM CITY** FOR
£300,000 FOR THE FIRST OF TWO SPELLS AT **UPTON PARK.**

7 1984: A £200,000 SIGNING FROM **FULHAM,** HE SPENT A DECADE
WITH **WEST HAM** BEFORE SPENDING A SEASON WITH **BLACKBURN
ROVERS,** WITH WHOM HE WON A LEAGUE TITLE AT THE AGE OF 35.

HE COULD'VE BEEN
A CONTENDER

AS A YOUNGSTER, *JUSTIN FASHANU* EXCELLED AT BOXING AND WAS SAID TO HAVE CONSIDERED A CAREER IN THE SPORT BEFORE OPTING TO PURSUE FOOTBALL. THE FIRST BLACK PLAYER TO COMMAND A £1 MILLION TRANSFER FEE, HE WAS ALSO THE FIRST OPENLY GAY PROFESSIONAL FOOTBALLER, AND HAD TO ENDURE PREJUDICE IN THE TABLOIDS, FROM THE TERRACES AND IN THE DRESSING ROOM. *FASHANU* TOOK HIS OWN LIFE IN 1998.

1 **BRIAN CLOUGH** SIGNED **JUSTIN FASHANU** TO **NOTTINGHAM FOREST** FROM WHICH CLUB FOR £1 MILLION IN 1981?

2 WHO WAS THE MANAGER WHO TOOK HIM ON LOAN FROM **NOTTINGHAM FOREST** AT **SOUTHAMPTON** IN 1982?

3 IN LATE 1982, **HOWARD WILKINSON** SIGNED HIM TO WHICH CLUB?

4 MOVING TO **BRIGHTON & HOVE ALBION**, HE SUFFERED A SERIOUS KNEE INJURY. FOLLOWING SURGERY AND A SPELL IN STATESIDE SOCCER, HE SPENT A MONTH WITH WHICH ENGLISH TEAM BEFORE JOINING **WEST HAM** IN 1989?

5 FOLLOWING HIS SHORT-LIVED STAY WITH **WEST HAM**, HE WAS SIGNED BY MANAGER **FRANK CLARK** TO WHICH LONDON CLUB?

6 IN THE EARLY 1990S, HE PLAYED FOR AND WAS ASSISTANT MANAGER OF WHICH WEST COUNTRY TEAM?

7 **JUSTIN'S** BROTHER, **JOHN FASHANU**, WON THE FA CUP WITH WHICH TEAM?

THE BOYS OF 1980

A MEMBER OF THE **WEST HAM** SIDE THAT REACHED THE 1975 FA YOUTH CUP FINAL, **GEOFF PIKE** WENT ON TO MAKE 372 APPEARANCES FOR **THE HAMMERS**, GAINING AN FA CUP WINNERS MEDAL IN 1980 AND A RUNNERS-UP MEDAL IN THE LEAGUE CUP IN 1981, THE SAME YEAR THAT THE TEAM WAS PROMOTED BACK TO THE TOP FLIGHT. AFTER A DOZEN YEARS AT **UPTON PARK** HE MOVED ON TO **NOTTS COUNTY**.

WHICH CLUB DID THESE MEMBERS OF THAT 1980 FA CUP-WINNING TEAM JOIN AFTER LEAVING **WEST HAM**?

1 PHIL PARKES

2 RAY STEWART

3 FRANK LAMPARD

4 ALVIN MARTIN

5 ALAN DEVONSHIRE

6 PAUL ALLEN

7 DAVID CROSS

8 TREVOR BROOKING

9 PAUL BRUSH

TEAM MEMBERS **BILLY BONDS** AND **STUART PEARSON** RETIRED AFTER PLAYING FOR **WEST HAM**.

HAMMERS & POTTERS

AFTER 14 SEASONS WITH *THE HAMMERS*, DURING WHICH TIME HE WON THE FA CUP AND THE EUROPEAN CUP WINNERS' CUP AND BECAME A HAT-TRICK HERO WITH *ENGLAND'S* WORLD CUP-WINNING TEAM, 30-YEAR-OLD *GEOFF HURST* JOINED *STOKE CITY* IN 1972. THREE YEARS LATER, HE ENDED HIS FOOTBALL LEAGUE CAREER WITH A SEASON AT *WEST BROMWICH ALBION*. AFTER SPELLS PLAYING IN IRELAND AND THE USA, HE LAUNCHED HIS MANAGEMENT CAREER AT *TELFORD UNITED*.

NAME THESE OTHERS WHO PLAYED FOR *WEST HAM* AND *STOKE CITY*:

1 SIGNED FROM *SPURS* AS PART OF THE DEAL THAT TOOK *FRÉDÉRIC KANOUTÉ* IN THE OPPOSITE DIRECTION, LEFT-WINGER WHO SPENT SIX SEASONS WITH *THE HAMMERS*, WINNING PROMOTION TO THE PREMIER LEAGUE AND REACHING AN FA CUP FINAL. *WEST HAM* PLAYER OF THE YEAR IN 2004, HE JOINED *STOKE* IN 2008 AND WAS VOTED THEIR PLAYER OF THE YEAR IN 2010.

2 A PREMIER LEAGUE WINNER WITH *MANCHESTER UNITED* IN 2001, MIDFIELDER WHO JOINED *THE HAMMERS* IN 2004. A YEAR LATER HE JOINED *STOKE* AND SUBSEQUENTLY PLAYED FOR *NORWICH CITY*, *MILTON KEYNES DONS* AND *CAMBRIDGE UNITED* BEFORE ENDING HIS PLAYING DAYS AT *SOHAM TOWN RANGERS*.

3 *SCOTLAND* GOALKEEPER WHO LEFT *WEST HAM UNITED* FOR *STOKE CITY* IN 1963 AND SUBSEQUENTLY PLAYED FOR *MILLWALL* AND *SOUTHEND UNITED*.

4 CENTRE-BACK WHO PLAYED AND SCORED FOR *ENGLAND* AT THE 2010 WORLD CUP, HE CAPTAINED *WEST HAM* BEFORE JOINING *STOKE CITY* IN 2011.

5 *SENEGAL* INTERNATIONAL WHO BETWEEN 2005 AND 2014, WON PROMOTIONS WITH *WEST HAM* AND *HULL CITY*, AND PLAYED FOR *STOKE CITY*, *BOLTON WANDERERS* AND *NEWCASTLE UNITED*.

6 *"THE BAD BOY OF AUSTRIAN FOOTBALL,"* HE JOINED *WEST HAM* IN 2017 AFTER FOUR SEASONS WITH *STOKE CITY*. HE FINISHED THE 2018-19 SEASON AS THE CLUB'S TOP SCORER BEFORE HEADING OFF TO PLAY IN CHINA.

"THE TERMINATOR"

JULIAN DICKS SPENT TWO SPELLS WITH **WEST HAM**, EITHER SIDE OF A SEASON WITH **LIVERPOOL**. THE FOUR-TIME **HAMMER OF THE YEAR** WAS A FEARSOME, TOUGH-TACKLING RED CARD MAGNET. APPROPRIATELY ENOUGH, HIS 2000 TESTIMONIAL GAME, A FRIENDLY AGAINST **ATHLETIC BILBAO**, WAS MARKED BY A 17-PLAYER BRAWL.

IDENTIFY THESE OTHERS WHO PLAYED FOR **WEST HAM** AND **LIVERPOOL**:

1 **ENGLAND** WINGER WHO SPENT EIGHT SEASONS AT **MIDDLESBROUGH**, WHERE HE WON THE 2004 LEAGUE CUP AND WAS A UEFA CUP RUNNER-UP. HE PLAYED IN THE 2010 LEAGUE CUP FINAL WITH **ASTON VILLA**, BEFORE WINNING THE 2012 LEAGUE CUP WITH **LIVERPOOL**. HE THEN HAD TWO SEASONS AT **WEST HAM** BEFORE RETURNING TO **MIDDLESBROUGH**, WHERE PROMOTION TO THE PREMIER LEAGUE WAS FOLLOWED BY A RETURN TO THE CHAMPIONSHIP. HE ENDED HIS PLAYING CAREER WITH TWO SEASONS AT **BLACKBURN ROVERS**.

2 **GUINEA** INTERNATIONAL WHO MADE HIS REPUTATION IN FRANCE, HE BECAME A CULT HERO AT **LIVERPOOL** WHEN IN 1999, ON THE DAY AFTER THE DEATH OF HIS FATHER, HE SCORED THE WINNER AGAINST **THE HAMMERS** AND DROPPED TO HIS KNEES IN TEARS. HE JOINED **WEST HAM** A YEAR LATER BUT HIS STAY WAS AN UNHAPPY ONE AND HE MOVED ON TO TEAMS IN THE MIDDLE EAST.

3 ISRAELI INTERNATIONAL WHO PLAYED IN THE 2006 FA CUP FINAL WITH **WEST HAM**, MADE A CONTROVERSIAL SWITCH TO LIVERPOOL IN 2007 AND WON THE UEFA EUROPA LEAGUE WITH **CHELSEA** IN 2013.

4 SPANISH GOALKEEPER WHO LEFT **WEST HAM** AFTER SIX YEARS TO JOIN **LIVERPOOL** IN 2019.

5   *CAMEROON* LEGEND WHO JOINED *THE HAMMERS* IN LATE 2000 -- BUT BECAUSE HE HAD PLAYED A FIRST ROUND UEFA CUP GAME THAT SEASON, WHEN *LIVERPOOL* WON THE TOURNAMENT HE WAS ELIGIBLE FOR A WINNER'S MEDAL!

THREE LIONS IRONS

BOBBY MOORE MADE 108 APPEARANCES FOR **ENGLAND**, 90 OF THOSE AS CAPTAIN. HIS FINEST HOUR UNDOUBTEDLY CAME IN 1966 WHEN HE LED **"THE THREE LIONS"** TO VICTORY IN THE WORLD CUP FINAL. TECHNICALLY, **MOORE** IS NOT **WEST HAM'S** MOST-CAPPED **ENGLAND** PLAYER -- GOALKEEPER **PETER SHILTON**, WHO PLAYED 125 TIMES FOR THE NATIONAL TEAM, WAS ON THE BOOKS AT **WEST HAM** IN 1966. ALTHOUGH HE NEVER MADE A FIRST TEAM APPEARANCE WITH **THE HAMMERS**, HE WAS NAMED AS A SUBSTITUTE ON OCCASION.

IDENTIFY THESE **HAMMERS** CAPPED BY **ENGLAND**:

1 **106 CAPS** (1999-2014): **WEST HAM** (2), **CHELSEA** (104)

2 **81 CAPS** (1997-2011): **WEST HAM** (10), **LEEDS UNITED** (17), **MANCHESTER UNITED** (54)

3 **78 CAPS** (1987-1999): **NOTTINGHAM FOREST** (76), **WEST HAM** (2)

4 **75 CAPS** (2008-2017): **MANCHESTER CITY** (63), **TORINO** (8) **WEST HAM** (4)

5 **67 CAPS** (1966-1974): **WEST HAM** (33), **TOTTENHAM HOTSPUR** (34)

6 **56 CAPS** (2001-2010): **WEST HAM** (10), **CHELSEA** (46)

7 **53 CAPS** (1997-2010): **LIVERPOOL** (1), **ASTON VILLA** (3), **WEST HAM** (17), **MANCHESTER CITY** (13), **PORTSMOUTH** (19)

8 **49 CAPS** (1966-1972): **WEST HAM** (49)

9 **47 CAPS** (1974-1982: **WEST HAM** (47)

10 **35 CAPS** (2005-2014): **MIDDLESBROUGH** (23,) **ASTON VILLA** (4), **LIVERPOOL** (7), **WEST HAM** (1)

11   *34 CAPS* (2001-2015): *WEST HAM* (2),
TOTTENHAM HOTSPUR (5), *MANCHESTER UNITED* (27)

12   *33 CAPS* (1991-1998): *CRYSTAL PALACE* (4),
ARSENAL (27), *WEST HAM* (2)

13   *21 CAPS* (2003-2010): *BIRMINGHAM CITY* (7), *WEST HAM* (14)

14   *18 CAPS* (2003-2013): *CHARLTON ATHLETIC* (1),
CHELSEA (1), *NEWCASTLE UNITED* (1), *WEST HAM* (3),
TOTTENHAM HOTSPUR (12)

15   *17 CAPS* (1981-1986): *WEST HAM* (17)

16   *12 CAPS* (2001-2003): *WEST HAM* (11), *MANCHESTER CITY* (1)

THE WILD ROVER

HAVING LAUNCHED HIS CAREER AT *ARSENAL*, *DAVID BENTLEY* SPENT TIME ON LOAN AT *NORWICH CITY* BEFORE JOINING *BLACKBURN ROVERS*, AND THEN SIGNED FOR *TOTTENHAM* IN A £15 MILLION DEAL IN 2008. HE WAS ALREADY FALLING DOWN THE PECKING ORDER WHEN, FOLLOWING A WIN OVER *MANCHESTER CITY* THAT SECURED A TOP FOUR FINISH FOR *SPURS*, HE DUMPED A BUCKET OF WATER OVER MANAGER *HARRY REDKNAPP* DURING A LIVE TV INTERVIEW. LOAN MOVES TO *BIRMINGHAM CITY*, *WEST HAM* AND *FC ROSTOV* FOLLOWED, BEFORE HE ENDED UP BACK AT *BLACKBURN ROVERS* IN 2013. WITHIN A YEAR, THE DISILLUSIONED *ENGLAND* WINGER HAD QUIT FOOTBALL -- AT THE AGE OF 29 -- AND MOVED TO MARBELLA TO RUN HIS RESTAURANT BUSINESS.

NAME THESE OTHER *HAMMERS* WHO PLAYED FOR *BLACKBURN*:

1 A PREMIER LEAGUE WINNER WITH *BLACKBURN ROVERS* IN 1995, DEFENDER WHO JOINED *WEST HAM* TWO YEARS LATER. NAMED HAMMER OF THE YEAR IN 1999, HIS SEVEN SEASONS AT THE CLUB WERE BADLY DISRUPTED BY A KNEE INJURY. HE SIGNED FOR *FULHAM* IN 2004.

2 *SOUTH AFRICA* STRIKER SIGNED FROM *BLACKBURN* IN 2010, HE'D PREVIOUSLY WON HONOURS WITH *AJAX*, *CELTA* AND *PORTO*.

3 A DOUBLE WINNER WITH *ARSENAL* IN 1971, *ENGLAND* FORWARD WHO SPENT A SEASON AT *WEST HAM* -- IN WHICH HE FAILED TO SCORE IN 28 LEAGUE GAMES -- BEFORE ENDING HIS LEAGUE CAREER WITH SECOND-TIER *BLACKBURN ROVERS*.

4 DENMARK RIGHT-BACK WHO WON HONOURS WITH *ODENSE*, *HAMBURGER SV* AND *COPENHAGEN*, PLAYED IN AN FA CUP FINAL WITH *EVERTON*, SPENT A SEASON AT *BLACKBURN* AND SIGNED FOR *WEST HAM* ON SUMMER TRANSFER DEADLINE DAY IN 2010.

5 AUSTRALIAN WHO SPENT SIX SEASONS AT *MILLWALL*, SIX AT *BLACKBURN* AND THREE SEASONS AT *WEST HAM* BEFORE JOINING *EVERTON* IN 2009.

6 SCOTLAND INTERNATIONAL WHO WON HONOURS WITH *DUNDEE UNITED*, WHERE HE WAS CONVERTED FROM STRIKER TO CENTRAL DEFENDER, PLAYED FOR *DERBY COUNTY* AND *BLACKBURN*, AND SPENT SEVEN SEASONS WITH *WEST HAM* BEFORE JOINING *SOUTHAMPTON* IN 2007. SIX MONTHS LATER HE SIGNED FOR *RANGERS*, WHERE HE WON LEAGUE AND CUP HONOURS.

7 CAPPED 44 TIMES BY *AUSTRALIA*, WHERE HE BEGAN AND ENDED HIS PLAYING DAYS, IN A CAREER THAT TOOK HIM TO *ANDERLECHT, LENS, BLACKBURN* -- WITH WHOM HE WON A PREMIER LEAGUE IN 1995 -- *WEST HAM, SOUTHAMPTON* AND *WOLVES*.

8 SIGNED FROM *BOURNEMOUTH* IN 1992, MIDFIELDER WHO LEFT *WEST HAM* FOR *BLACKBURN* THREE YEARS LATER IN A £1.2 MILLION DEAL. A LEG INJURY WHILE PLAYING FOR *CHARLTON ATHLETIC* IN 1998 ENDED HIS CAREER.

HEY, BIG SPENDERS!

THE £7.5 MILLION **WEST HAM** PAID TO **LIVERPOOL** TO SIGN **CRAIG BELLAMY** IN THE SUMMER OF 2007 WAS A CLUB RECORD AT THE TIME -- BUT BY OCTOBER, INJURY HAD RULED THE **WALES** INTERNATIONAL OUT FOR THE REST OF THE SEASON. THE 2008-09 SEASON WAS UNDERWAY BEFORE HE RETURNED -- AND IN THE JANUARY TRANSFER WINDOW, **THE HAMMERS** ACCEPTED A £14 MILLION OFFER FROM **MANCHESTER CITY**.

IDENTIFY THESE OTHER CLUB RECORD SIGNINGS:

1 1993: **RANGERS** £750,000

2 1994: **OXFORD UNITED** £1.2 MILLION

3 1996: **ESPANYOL** £2.2 MILLION

4 1997: **ARSENAL** £3.2 MILLION

5 1999: **LENS** £4.2 MILLION

6 2001: **SUNDERLAND** £5 MILLION

7 2001: **FIORENTINA** £5.5 MILLION

8 2006: **NORWICH CITY** £7.25 MILLION

9 2009: **BRESCIA** £9 MILLION

10 2012: **WOLVES** £10.75 MILLION

11 2013: **LIVERPOOL** £15.5 MILLION

12 2016: **SWANSEA CITY** £20.5 MILLION

13 2018: **TOULOUSE** £22 MILLION

14 2018: **LAZIO** £36 MILLION

REGGAE BOYZ RECRUIT

WEST HAM'S ALL-TIME TOP SCORER IN THE PREMIER LEAGUE, **MICHAIL ANTONIO** LAUNCHED HIS CAREER AT NON-LEAGUE **TOOTING & MITCHAM UNITED** AND WORKED HIS WAY UP THROUGH THE LEAGUES TO FINALLY GAIN TOP-FLIGHT SUCCESS.

ANTONIO CAME CLOSE TO PLAYING FOR **ENGLAND**, BEING AN UNUSED SUBSTITUTE UNDER **SAM ALLARDYCE** AND HAVING TO PULL OUT OF A **GARETH SOUTHGATE** SQUAD THROUGH INJURY, BUT HAVING OBTAINED A JAMAICAN PASSPORT, HE MADE HIS DEBUT FOR **JAMAICA** IN 2021.

WHICH CARIBBEAN COUNTRY HAVE THE FOLLOWING REPRESENTED?

1 SHAKA HISLOP

2 RAVEL MORRISON

3 MOSES ASHIKODI

4 ADAM NEWTON

5 JULIEN FAUBERT

6 BRENT RAHIM

7 FRÉDÉRIC PIQUIONNE

8 SÉBASTIEN CAROLE

9 CLYDE BEST

10 JOBI MCANUFF

THE GOLDEN BOYS

WEST HAM LEGEND **BOBBY MOORE** WON NUMEROUS HONOURS IN HIS GLITTERING CAREER, INCLUDING THE BBC SPORTS PERSONALITY OF THE YEAR AND THE FWA FOOTBALLER OF THE YEAR.

HE WAS AN INAUGURAL INDUCTEE OF THE ENGLISH FOOTBALL HALL OF FAME IN 2002. NAME THESE OTHER **WEST HAM** INDUCTEES BY THE YEAR THEY WERE INDUCTED, THE ENGLISH TEAMS THEY PLAYED FOR AND NUMBER OF APPEARANCES FOR THOSE TEAMS:

1 2002: *CHELSEA* (157), *TOTTENHAM HOTSPUR* (321), *WEST HAM* (38)

2 2004: *WEST HAM* (411), *STOKE CITY* (108), *WEST BROMWICH ALBION* (10)

3 2005: *CRYSTAL PALACE* (225), *ARSENAL* (221), *WEST HAM* (22), *NOTTINGHAM FOREST* (10), *BURNLEY* (15)

4 2006: *ARSENAL* (235), *WEST HAM* (89)

5 2006: *WEST HAM* (302), *TOTTENHAM HOTSPUR* (189), *NORWICH CITY* (207), *SHEFFIELD UNITED* (24)

6 2009: *WEST HAM* (528)

7 2009: *MILLWALL* (220), *ALDERSHOT* (5), *NOTTINGHAM FOREST* (42), *TOTTENHAM HOTSPUR* (236), *MANCHESTER UNITED* (104), *PORTSMOUTH* (32), *WEST HAM* (76), *COLCHESTER UNITED* (19)

8 2015: *COVENTRY CITY* (52), *NOTTINGHAM FOREST* (402), *NEWCASTLE UNITED* (37), *WEST HAM* (42), *MANCHESTER CITY* (38)

9 2016: *WEST HAM* (127), *BOURNEMOUTH* (10), *LEEDS UNITED* (54), *MANCHESTER UNITED* (312), *QUEENS PARK RANGERS* (11)

10 2017: *WEST HAM* (148), *SWANSEA CITY* (9), *CHELSEA* (429), *MANCHESTER CITY* (32)

11 2020: *NORWICH CITY* (90), *NOTTINGHAM FOREST* (32), *SOUTHAMPTON* (9), *NOTTS COUNTY* (64), *BRIGHTON & HOVE ALBION* (16), *MANCHESTER CITY* (2), *WEST HAM* (2), *LEYTON ORIENT* (5), *TORQUAY UNITED* (41)

THE CONVEYOR BELT

THE 20TH PLAYER TO SCORE A CENTURY OF PREMIER LEAGUE GOALS, **JERMAIN DEFOE** WON THE FIRST LEAGUE TITLE IN HIS CAREER AT THE AGE OF 38. AS A YOUNGSTER, HE PLAYED HIS FOOTBALL WITH **SENRAB** -- THE NAME IS BARNES SPELLED BACKWARDS -- THE NON-LEAGUE SIDE THAT HAS PRODUCED A STEADY STREAM OF TOP FLIGHT PLAYERS AND COACHES, A NUMBER OF WHOM JOINED **WEST HAM.**

IDENTIFY THE FOLLOWING **SENRAB** ALUMNI BY THE TEAMS THEY SUBSEQUENTLY PLAYED FOR OR MANAGED:

1 *CHARLTON ATHLETIC, LEEDS UNITED, WEST HAM* (TWICE), *NEWCASTLE UNITED, BIRMINGHAM CITY, IPSWICH TOWN* (1994-2012) BEFORE MANAGING *CHARLTON ATHLETIC* AND *BIRMINGHAM CITY*

2 *BRISTOL ROVERS, BATH CITY, BRIGHTON & HOVE ALBION* (TWICE), *TOTTENHAM HOTSPUR, WEST HAM, FULHAM, QUEENS PARK RANGERS* (1999-2016)

3   **WEST HAM, BIRMINGHAM CITY, ASTON VILLA, CHARLTON ATHLETIC** (TWICE), **BRIGHTON & HOVE ALBION** (1975-93) THEN MANAGED **CHARLTON ATHLETIC** AND **WEST HAM**

4   **WEST HAM** AND **BARNET** (1969-72) BEFORE 43 YEARS OF SERVICE AT **WEST HAM**, PRIMARILY AS ACADEMY DIRECTOR

5   **CHARLTON ATHLETIC, TOTTENHAM HOTSPUR, WEST HAM, FULHAM, LIVERPOOL, NOTTINGHAM FOREST, LEICESTER CITY, QUEENS PARK RANGERS, GILLINGHAM, BILLERICAY TOWN** (TWICE), **EAST THURROCK UNITED** (1997-2020)

MANUEL'S MEN

ŁUKASZ FABIAŃSKI WAS BROUGHT TO **WEST HAM** BY **MANUEL PELLEGRINI** IN 2018. THE FIRST POLE TO PLAY FOR **THE HAMMERS**, THE GOALKEEPER WAS A £7 MILLION SIGNING FROM **SWANSEA CITY**.

FROM WHICH CLUBS WERE THESE **PELLEGRINI** SIGNINGS ACQUIRED?

1 ISSA DIOP

2 ANDRIY YARMOLENKO

3 SÉBASTIEN HALLER

4 PABLO FORNALS

5 ALBIAN AJETI

6 FELIPE ANDERSON

7 LUCAS PÉREZ

8 FABIÁN BALBUENA

9 RYAN FREDERICKS

10 JACK WILSHERE

11 CARLOS SÁNCHEZ

12 ROBERTO

13 DAVID MARTIN

THE NAME IS BOND...
JOHN BOND

A MEMBER OF THE **WEST HAM** TEAM THAT WON PROMOTION IN 1958 AND AN FA CUP WINNER IN 1964, **JOHN BOND** PLAYED 381 LEAGUE GAMES BEFORE ENDING HIS PLAYING DAYS AT **TORQUAY UNITED**, HELPING THE CLUB TO A PROMOTION. HE WENT ON TO MANAGE **BOURNEMOUTH**, **NORWICH CITY, MANCHESTER CITY, BURNLEY, SWANSEA CITY, BIRMINGHAM CITY, SHREWSBURY TOWN** AND **WITTON ALBION**.

WHICH FORMER **HAMMER** WENT ON TO MANAGE:

1 BRISTOL ROVERS, COVENTRY CITY, WIMBLEDON, WEST BROMWICH ALBION, WALES, CARDIFF CITY, CHELTENHAM TOWN, WEYMOUTH, WANDERERS

2 GLOUCESTER CITY, MERTHYR TYDFIL, TORQUAY UNITED, BRENTFORD, SIERRA LEONE

3 HAJDUK SPLIT, CIBALIA, NK ZAGREB, CROATIA, ZADAR, SEPAHAN, AL-SHAHANIA, INDIA

4 WEYMOUTH, TORQUAY UNITED, LEICESTER CITY, MANCHESTER UNITED, CARDIFF CITY, IRAN, AL-SHAAB

5 MANCHESTER CITY, ENGLAND U21, GREAT BRITAIN, NOTTINGHAM FOREST

6 MACCLESFIELD TOWN, MILTON KEYNES DONS, BLACKBURN ROVERS, NOTTS COUNTY, BLACKPOOL

7 NEWCASTLE UNITED, BIRMINGHAM CITY, NORWICH CITY, BRIGHTON & HOVE ALBION, NOTTINGHAM FOREST

8 OLDHAM ATHLETIC, CRYSTAL PALACE, CHARLTON ATHLETIC, COVENTRY CITY, QUEENS PARK RANGERS

9 COVENTRY CITY, PETERBOROUGH UNITED, NEW ENGLAND TEA MEN, JACKSONVILLE TEA MEN

10 *NORWICH CITY, SHREWSBURY TOWN, PLYMOUTH ARGYLE*

11 *BATH CITY, TORONTO CITY, PLYMOUTH ARGYLE,
MANCHESTER CITY, GALATASARAY, YEOVIL TOWN,
SPORTING CP, MIDDLESBROUGH, WILLINGTON, KUWAIT,
VITÓRIA DE SETÚBAL, SC FARENSE, FISHER ATHLETIC,
BRISTOL ROVERS*

12 *BARNET, BRENTFORD, MILTON KEYNES DONS, LEICESTER
CITY, CHELTENHAM TOWN, NOTTS COUNTY, GILLINGHAM,
EASTLEIGH, CHESTERFIELD*

MAN U MEN

MANCHESTER UNITED SWOOPED TO SIGN GUADALAJARA'S JAVIER HERNÁNDEZ AHEAD OF THE 2010 WORLD CUP, A MOVE THAT WAS BORNE OUT BY HIS GOALSCORING PERFORMANCES FOR MEXICO IN THE TOURNAMENT. IN SIX SEASONS AT OLD TRAFFORD, "CHICHARITO" -- HIS NICKNAME MEANS "LITTLE PEA" IN SPANISH -- WON TWO LEAGUE TITLES. TOWARDS THE END OF HIS UNITED DAYS, HE WON THE FIFA CLUB WORLD CUP ON LOAN AT REAL MADRID, BEFORE SPENDING TWO SEASONS AT BAYER LEVERKUSEN. HE JOINED WEST HAM IN 2017, BEFORE MOVING ON TO SEVILLA THREE SEASONS LATER. 2020 SAW HIM HEAD TO THE STATES TO SIGN FOR LA GALAXY.

NAME THESE OTHER HAMMERS WHO PLAYED FOR THE RED DEVILS:

1   ENGLAND MIDFIELDER WHO SCORED 9 GOALS AND MADE FIVE ASSISTS IN 16 GAMES WHILE ON LOAN AT WEST HAM IN 2020-21.

2   ARGENTINA FORWARD WHO LEFT WEST HAM FOR MANCHESTER UNITED IN 2007.

3   REPUBLIC OF IRELAND FULL-BACK WHO CAPTAINED THE HAMMERS TO A FIRST TOP FLIGHT PROMOTION IN 26 YEARS IN 1958 AND CAPTAINED UNITED TO FA CUP FINAL VICTORY IN 1963.

4   FRENCH STRIKER WHO JOINED UNITED FROM SUNDERLAND IN 2003 AND SPENT THE FIRST HALF OF THE 2006-07 SEASON ON LOAN AT WEST HAM.

5   UNITED STATES DEFENDER WHO JOINED THE HAMMERS FROM UNITED IN 2006. HE WAS WITH THE CLUB FOR FIVE SEASONS, BEFORE DROPPING DOWN A DIVISION TO JOIN BIRMINGHAM CITY, WHERE HE PLAYED FOR SIX YEARS BEFORE RETURNING TO AMERICA TO JOIN ORLANDO CITY.

6   DUTCH GOALKEEPER WHO WON UEFA CHAMPIONS LEAGUE, FA CUP AND TWO PREMIER LEAGUE MEDALS WITH UNITED BEFORE HIS 2002 MOVE TO WEST HAM. HE DIDN'T PLAY A COMPETITIVE GAME FOR THE HAMMERS AND RETURNED TO DUTCH FOOTBALL IN 2003.

7 **NORTHERN IRELAND** GOALKEEPER WHO WON HONOURS WITH **UNITED** AND **OLYMPIACOS**, HIS CLUBS INCLUDED **WIGAN ATHLETIC, HULL CITY, DERBY COUNTY** AND **NOTTS COUNTY** AND A TWO-YEAR SPELL WITH **WEST HAM** BETWEEN 2005 AND 2007.

8 STRIKER -- NICKNAMED **"PANCHO"** -- WHO BEGAN HIS CAREER AT **HULL CITY**, WON THE 1975 SECOND DIVISION TITLE AND 1977 FA CUP WITH **UNITED**, AND THE 1980 FA CUP WITH **WEST HAM**.

ALLEZ LES BLEUS!

SAMIR NASRI WAS A MEMBER OF THE **FRANCE** TEAM THAT WON THE 2004 UEFA EUROPEAN UNDER-17 CHAMPIONSHIP AND WENT ON TO WIN 41 CAPS AT SENIOR LEVEL. HE RETIRED FROM INTERNATIONAL FOOTBALL AT THE AGE OF 27 AFTER BEING OMITTED FROM THE 2014 WORLD CUP SQUAD.

IDENTIFY THESE OTHER **FRANCE** INTERNATIONALS WHO HAVE PLAYED FOR **WEST HAM UNITED**:

1 GOALKEEPER WHO WAS A MEMBER OF THE SQUADS THAT WON THE 1998 WORLD CUP AND EURO 2000, HE PLAYED FOR **THE HAMMERS** ON LOAN FROM **PARIS SAINT-GERMAIN** IN EARLY 1998.

2 MIDFIELDER WHO WON INTERTOTO CUPS WITH **STRASBOURG** AND **WEST HAM**, HE SIGNED FOR **THE HAMMERS** IN 1998 AND MOVED ON TO **BLACKBURN ROVERS** IN EARLY 2001 AFTER SPENDING A SHORT TIME ON LOAN AT **PORTSMOUTH**.

3 CAPPED 44 TIMES BY **FRANCE**, FOR WHOM HE PLAYED AT THE 2006 AND 2010 WORLD CUP TOURNAMENTS, MIDFIELDER WHO WON HONOURS WITH **LENS, LYON, BORDEAUX** AND **MARSEILLE**, BUT HAD UNSUCCESSFUL SPELLS IN ENGLAND WITH **LIVERPOOL, WEST HAM** AND **CHARLTON ATHLETIC**.

4 MIDFIELDER WHO JOINED **WEST HAM** FROM **MARSEILLE** IN 2014, HAVING PLAYED ON LOAN AT **WEST BROMWICH ALBION** THE PREVIOUS SEASON, HIS ONLY **FRANCE** CAP CAME IN 2012.

5 A £10.7 MILLION SIGNING TO **WEST HAM** FROM **MARSEILLE** IN 2015, HE WON THE **HAMMER OF THE YEAR** AWARD BEFORE AN ACRIMONIOUS £25 MILLION RETURN TO **MARSEILLE** IN 2017.

6 LEFT-BACK CAPPED 81 TIMES, HE WON A MULTITUDE OF HONOURS WITH **MONACO, MANCHESTER UNITED** -- INCLUDING THE 2008 UEFA CHAMPIONS LEAGUE -- AND **JUVENTUS** BEFORE ENDING HIS PLAYING DAYS WITH A BRIEF SPELL AT **WEST HAM** IN 2018.

7 CENTRE-BACK SIGNED TO **THE HAMMERS** FROM **CHELSEA** IN 2021 AFTER LOANS AT **STOKE CITY** AND **EVERTON**.

8 **PARIS SAINT-GERMAIN** GOALKEEPER WHO JOINED **WEST HAM** ON LOAN IN 2021 AFTER LOAN SPELLS AT **REAL MADRID** AND **FULHAM.**

GO WEST, YOUNG MAN

RIO FERDINAND MADE HIS *WEST HAM* DEBUT AT THE AGE OF 17 AT THE TAIL END OF THE 1995-96 SEASON. THE NEXT SEASON SAW HIM SPEND A TIME ON LOAN AT *BOURNEMOUTH*, PLAYING 11 GAMES FOR THE DORSET CLUB BEFORE RETURNING TO *UPTON PARK*. DURING THE 1997-98 SEASON, HE WON THE *HAMMER OF THE YEAR* AWARD AT THE AGE OF 19!

IDENTIFY THESE OTHER *HAMMERS* WHO PLAYED FOR *BOURNEMOUTH:*

1 MIDFIELDER WHO PLAYED FOR BOTH TEAMS AND LATER MANAGED BOTH TEAMS!

2 *WALES* MIDFIELDER WHO HELPED *BOURNEMOUTH* WIN A PROMOTION IN 2003 BEFORE MOVING ON TO *WEST HAM* A YEAR LATER -- AND *THE HAMMERS* WERE PROMOTED TO THE TOP FLIGHT IN HIS DEBUT SEASON. HE LATER MOVED ON TO *CHARLTON ATHLETIC* AND WAS EVENTUALLY MANAGER OF *PLYMOUTH ARGYLE* AND *LEYTON ORIENT*.

3 CAPPED 15 TIMES BY *WALES*, MIDFIELDER WHO CAME THROUGH THE RANKS AT *WEST HAM* AND MADE 121 APPEARANCES BETWEEN 2007 AND 2014, SPENDING TIME ON LOAN AT *BOURNEMOUTH* AND *WIGAN ATHLETIC* IN HIS FINAL SEASON WITH *THE HAMMERS*. INJURY CURTAILED HIS CAREER AND HE WENT INTO COACHING.

4 MIDFIELDER WHO WON PROMOTION TO THE TOP FLIGHT IN HIS FIRST SEASON WITH *WEST HAM* FOLLOWING HIS 1992 SWITCH FROM *BOURNEMOUTH*. HE BRIEFLY PLAYED FOR *BLACKBURN ROVERS* BEFORE JOINING *CHARLTON ATHLETIC* BUT HIS CAREER WAS ENDED BY A *KEVIN MUSCAT* TACKLE IN EARLY 1998.

5 HIS DECADE WITH *SPURS* EARNED THE WINGER A LEAGUE CUP WINNER'S MEDAL IN 1971 BEFORE HE SPENT THREE YEARS WITH *NORWICH CITY*. A SOJOURN IN THE STATES WITH *SEATTLE SOUNDERS* WAS FOLLOWED BY HIS 1979 MOVE TO *WEST HAM*. TOWARDS THE END OF HIS FOUR YEARS AT *UPTON PARK*, HE SPENT TIME ON LOAN AT *BOURNEMOUTH*, BEFORE TAKING UP A COACHING CAREER.

6 CAPPED 46 TIMES BY **NORTHERN IRELAND**, STRIKER WHOSE LENGTHY LIST OF CLUBS INCLUDES **BLACKBURN ROVERS.** HE WON PROMOTIONS WITH **SWINDON TOWN, WEST HAM** AND **READING**, WAS THE DIVISION TWO GOLDEN BOOT WINNER IN 1994 AND PLAYED FOR AND LATER MANAGED **BOURNEMOUTH.**

THE SOUTH AMERICANS

A FORMER MEMBER OF COSTA RICA'S NATIONAL YOUTH BASKETBALL TEAM, **PAULO WANCHOPE** LAUNCHED HIS FOOTBALL CAREER WITH **CS HEREDIANO** AND ARRIVED IN ENGLAND AS A 20-YEAR-OLD TO PLAY FOR **DERBY COUNTY**. TWO YEARS LATER, HE SIGNED FOR **WEST HAM UNITED**, AND A SEASON LATER, HE JOINED **MANCHESTER CITY**. HE SUBSEQUENTLY PLAYED FOR CLUBS IN SPAIN, QATAR, COSTA RICA, ARGENTINA, JAPAN AND THE UNITED STATES BEFORE RETIRING. HE SCORED 45 GOALS IN 73 GAMES FOR **COSTA RICA**.

FROM WHICH SOUTH AMERICAN COUNTRIES DO THESE **HAMMERS** HAIL?

1 **WÁLTER LÓPEZ**

2 **MANUEL LANZINI**

3 **BRIAN MONTENEGRO**

4 **JAVIER MARGAS**

5 **NOLBERTO SOLANO**

6 **ENNER VALENCIA**

7 **WELLINGTON PAULISTA**

8 **FABIÁN BALBUENA**

9 **PABLO ARMERO**

10 **LIONEL SCALONI**

11 **CARLOS SÁNCHEZ**

12 **LUIS JIMÉNEZ**

TOFFEE HAMMERS!

NICLAS ALEXANDERSSON LAUNCHED HIS CAREER AT **VESSIGEBRO BK**, MOVING ON TO **HALMSTADS BK** AND **IFK GÖTEBORG**, BEFORE JOINING **SHEFFIELD WEDNESDAY** IN 1997. THE SWEDISH INTERNATIONAL MIDFIELDER -- HE MADE 109 APPEARANCES FOR HIS COUNTRY -- JOINED **EVERTON** IN THE SUMMER OF 2000. A BRIEF LOAN PERIOD AT **WEST HAM** IN 2003 WAS FOLLOWED BY A RETURN TO **IFK GÖTEBORG**, WHERE HE PLAYED FOR FIVE SEASONS BEFORE RETIRING IN 2009.

IDENTIFY THESE **HAMMERS** WITH **EVERTON** LINKS:

1 **FRANCE** CENTRE-BACK WHO JOINED **WEST HAM** FROM **CHELSEA** IN 2021 FOLLOWING LOAN SPELLS WITH **STOKE** AND **EVERTON**.

2 **SCOTLAND** MIDFIELDER WHO HAD TWO SPELLS WITH **WEST HAM** -- IN 1994-96 AND 2001-2005 -- PLAYED FOR **EVERTON** AND **LIVERPOOL**, **SUNDERLAND**, **MILLWALL**, **LUTON** AND MORE.

3 **AUSTRALIA** DEFENDER WHO HAD LENGTHY SPELLS WITH **MILLWALL** AND **BLACKBURN ROVERS**, CAPTAINED **WEST HAM**, JOINED **EVERTON** IN 2007 AND LATER PLAYED IN TURKEY, ABU DHABI, DUBAI AND JAPAN BEFORE WINDING DOWN HIS CAREER AT **WATFORD** AND **DONCASTER ROVERS** IN 2014.

4 STRIKER WHO JOINED **EVERTON** IN A RECORD £2.2 MILLION DEAL IN 1988 AFTER SIX SEASONS WITH **WEST HAM**. HE SPENT SIX SEASONS ON MERSEYSIDE BEFORE RETURNING TO **WEST HAM**. HE SUBSEQUENTLY WON A LEAGUE CUP WITH **LEICESTER CITY** AND LATER PLAYED FOR **BIRMINGHAM CITY**, **NORWICH CITY**, **BARNET** AND **MILLWALL**.

5 AN FA CUP WINNER WITH **EVERTON** IN 1995, HE SPENT A SEASON AT **WEST HAM** AND A MONTH AT **ASTON VILLA** BEFORE RETURNING TO **EVERTON** IN 1998. HE SUBSEQUENTLY PLAYED FOR A NUMBER OF OTHER CLUBS BEFORE MOVING INTO COACHING AND WAS LATER CARETAKER MANAGER AT **PRESTON NORTH END** AND **EVERTON**.

6 **ECUADOR** FORWARD SIGNED TO **WEST HAM** FROM MEXICO'S **PACHUCA**, HE SPENT A SEASON ON LOAN AT **EVERTON** IN 2016-17.

7   *ENGLAND* GOALKEEPER WHOSE CLUBS INCLUDE *ARSENAL, EVERTON AND WEST HAM,* HE SPENT THREE SEPARATE SPELLS AT *IPSWICH TOWN.*

8   *CROATIA* MIDFIELDER WHO LEFT *EVERTON* FOR *CSKA MOSCOW* IN 2018 AND SIGNED FOR *WEST HAM* IN 2021.

9   *CROATIA* DEFENDER WHO PLAYED FOR BOTH *EVERTON* AND *WEST HAM* AND LATER MANAGED *THE HAMMERS.*

10   *DENMARK* RIGHT-BACK WHO PLAYED IN DENMARK, GERMANY AND FRANCE, HE PLAYED FOR *EVERTON* AND *BLACKBURN ROVERS* BEFORE JOINING *WEST HAM* IN 2010.

BIG MAL

AFTER SEVEN SEASONS AT *CHARLTON ATHLETIC, MALCOLM ALLISON* JOINED *WEST HAM* IN 1951. HIS PLAYING CAREER WAS DERAILED IN 1957 AFTER A BOUT OF TUBERCULOSIS RESULTED IN THE REMOVAL OF A LUNG. HE WAS ALREADY IMMERSED IN TACTICS AND COACHING METHODS AND HAD MENTORED A NUMBER OF YOUNGER PLAYERS AT THE CLUB, WHICH STOOD HIM IN GOOD STEAD FOR HIS SUBSEQUENT COACHING CAREER. A MAVERICK, CONTROVERSIAL, LARGER-THAN-LIFE CHARACTER, HE MANAGED CLUB TEAMS IN ENGLAND, CANADA, PORTUGAL AND TURKEY AND THE *KUWAIT* NATIONAL TEAM.

WHICH NATIONAL TEAM DID THE FORMER *WEST HAM* MANAGER OR PLAYER COACH IN THE TIME PERIOD SHOWN?

1 *SIERRA LEONE* (2007)

2 *IRAN* (1974-1976)

3 *WALES* (1995-1999)

4 *CROATIA* (2012-2013)

5 *ENGLAND* (1977-1982)

6 *KENYA* (2006)

7 *JORDAN* (2016)

8 *INDIA* (2019-)

9 *ISRAEL* (2002-2006)

10 *REPUBLIC OF IRELAND* (1953-1967)

11 *COSTA RICA* (2014-2015)

12 *GHANA* (2014-2017)

MANAGERIAL MERRY-GO-ROUNDS

HAVING WON 24 **SCOTLAND** CAPS AND A MULTITUDE OF HONOURS WITH **CELTIC** AND **MANCHESTER UNITED**, **LOU MACARI** WOUND DOWN HIS PLAYING DAYS WHILE ALSO LAUNCHING HIS MANAGEMENT CAREER WITH **SWINDON TOWN**. TWO PROMOTIONS WITH THE WILTSHIRE CLUB HELPED EARN HIM THE **WEST HAM** MANAGER JOB IN 1989 - THE FIRST WITHOUT ANY PRIOR CONNECTIONS TO THE CLUB EVER APPOINTED. HIS TENURE WAS BRIEF AND HE WAS GONE BY EARLY 1990. HE WENT ON TO MANAGE **STOKE CITY** TWICE, **BIRMINGHAM CITY**, **CELTIC** AND **HUDDERSFIELD TOWN**.

IDENTIFY THESE **WEST HAM** BOSSES BY OTHER TEAMS THEY MANAGED:

1 *HAPOEL PETAH TIKVA, MACCABI TEL AVIV, HAPOEL HAIFA, MACCABI HAIFA, ISRAEL, CHELSEA, PORTSMOUTH, PARTIZAN BELGRADE, GHANA, NORTHEAST UNITED*

2 *ITALY U16, WATFORD, CAGLIARI, AL-ARABI, BIRMINGHAM CITY*

3 *BOURNEMOUTH, PORTSMOUTH, SOUTHAMPTON, TOTTENHAM HOTSPUR, QUEENS PARK RANGERS, JORDAN, BIRMINGHAM CITY*

4 *GILLINGHAM, WATFORD, NEWCASTLE UNITED, NORWICH CITY, STEVENAGE*

5 *READING, CHARLTON ATHLETIC, SOUTHAMPTON, NEWCASTLE UNITED, CRYSTAL PALACE, WEST BROMWICH ALBION, ADO DEN HAAG*

6 *LIMERICK, PRESTON NORTH END* (CARETAKER), *BLACKPOOL, NOTTS COUNTY, BOLTON WANDERERS, NEWCASTLE UNITED, BLACKBURN ROVERS, SUNDERLAND, ENGLAND, CRYSTAL PALACE, EVERTON, WEST BROMWICH ALBION*

7   *HAJDUK SPLIT, CROATIA U21, CROATIA, LOKOMOTIV MOSCOW, BEŞIKTAŞ, AL-ITTIHAD, WEST BROMWICH ALBION, BEIJING GUOAN*

8   *PRESTON NORTH END, EVERTON, MANCHESTER UNITED, REAL SOCIEDAD, SUNDERLAND*

9   *UNIVERSIDAD DE CHILE, PALETINO, O'HIGGINS, UNIVERSIDAD CATÓLICA, LDU QUITO, SAN LORENZO, RIVER PLATE, VILLARREAL, REAL MADRID, MÁLAGA, MANCHESTER CITY, HEBEI CHINA FORTUNE, REAL BETIS*

LAST LINE OF DEFENCE

JOE HART MADE 75 APPEARANCES FOR ENGLAND, FOUR OF THEM WHILE ON THE BOOKS AT WEST HAM. HART KEPT A CLEAN SHEET IN 43 OF THE GAMES IN WHICH HE PLAYED, THE SECOND-HIGHEST TALLY OF ANY ENGLAND GOALKEEPER.

WHICH COUNTRIES DID THE FOLLOWING WEST HAM GOALKEEPERS REPRESENT AT INTERNATIONAL LEVEL?

1 DAVID JAMES 1997-2010

2 LAWRIE LESLIE 1960-1961

3 CRAIG FORREST 1988-2002

4 PAVEL SRNÍČEK 1994-2001

5 BOBBY FERGUSON 1965-1966

6 PHIL PARKES 1974

7 ALLEN MCKNIGHT 1987-1989

8 BERNARD LAMA 1993-2000

9 SHAKA HISLOP 1999-2006

10 SAŠA ILIĆ 1998-2001

11 IAN FEUER 1992

12 ROY CARROLL 1997-2017

13 ROBERT GREEN 2005-2012

14 JUSSI JÄÄSKELÄINEN 1998-2010

MAKING AN ENTRANCE!

JIMMY GREAVES WAS RENOWNED FOR SCORING IN HIS FIRST GAME FOR EVERY CLUB HE PLAYED FOR. HIS **WEST HAM** DEBUT IN 1970 WAS NO EXCEPTION -- HE SCORED TWICE IN A 5-1 WIN AGAINST **MANCHESTER CITY** AT **MAINE ROAD**.

NAME THESE OTHER GOALSCORING DEBUTS FOR **WEST HAM**:

1 1988: SIGNED FROM **ARSENAL**, SCORED THE ONLY GOAL IN A 1-0 WIN OVER **SHEFFIELD WEDNESDAY** AT **HILLSBOROUGH**.

2 2015: SCORED AGAINST **ASTRA GIURGIU** IN ROMANIA IN A UEFA EUROPA LEAGUE QUALIFIER JUST THREE MINUTES INTO HIS DEBUT AFTER ARRIVING AT **WEST HAM** FROM **AL JAZIRA CLUB**.

3 1947: SCORED A HAT-TRICK IN A 4-0 HOME VICTORY OVER **CHESTERFIELD**.

4 1983: HOME-GROWN STRIKER WHO WAS ONLY 17 WHEN HE HEADED HOME THE OPENER IN A 3-0 WIN OVER **TOTTENHAM HOTSPUR** ON NEW YEAR'S DAY, THE FIRST OF HIS 146 GOALS FOR THE CLUB.

5 2006: **CHELSEA** PRODIGY WHO HAD SPENT TIME ON LOAN AT **WOLVES, CHARLTON ATHLETIC** AND **ASTON VILLA**, HE SCORED JUST SECONDS AFTER COMING ON AGAINST **CHARLTON ATHLETIC**, A GAME THAT RESULTED IN A 3-1 WIN.

6 2021: LOAN SIGNING FROM **MANCHESTER UNITED** WHO SCORED TWICE ON HIS DEBUT FOR **THE HAMMERS** IN A 3-1 AWAY WIN AT **ASTON VILLA**.

7 2008: 18-YEAR-OLD WHO CAME ON AS A SUBSTITUTE AGAINST **BLACKBURN ROVERS** AND SCORED THE WINNER JUST FIVE MINUTES AND 16 SECONDS INTO HIS SENIOR CAREER.

CURBS YOUR ENTHUSIASM

AFTER NINE YEARS WITH **ARSENAL,** DURING WHICH TIME HE WON TWO LEAGUE TITLES AND THREE FA CUPS -- INCLUDING THE DOUBLE IN 2002 -- **SWEDEN** CAPTAIN **FREDDIE LJUNGBERG** JOINED **WEST HAM** IN A FOUR-YEAR DEAL. HOWEVER, HIS **HAMMERS** SOJOURN ENDED AFTER ONE INJURY-HIT SEASON AND HE HEADED STATESIDE TO PLAY IN THE MLS.

LJUNGBERG WAS AN **ALAN CURBISHLEY** SIGNING, AS WERE THE FOLLOWING. FROM WHICH CLUBS WERE THEY SIGNED?:

1 *MATTHEW UPSON*

2 *KIERON DYER*

3 *CRAIG BELLAMY*

4 *SCOTT PARKER*

5 *JULIEN FAUBERT*

6 *LUÍS BOA MORTE*

7 *VALON BEHRAMI*

8 *CALUM DAVENPORT*

9 *LUCAS NEILL*

10 *NIGEL QUASHIE*

11 *DAVID DI MICHELE*

12 *KEPA BLANCO*

13 *RICHARD WRIGHT*

14 *HENRI CAMARA*

15 *NOLBERTO SOLANO*

DUTY CALLS

19-YEAR-OLD *JOE COLE* MADE HIS *ENGLAND* DEBUT IN A 4-0 VICTORY OVER *MEXICO* IN MAY OF 2001. IT WAS THE FIRST OF 56 GAMES FOR HIS COUNTRY, IN WHICH HE SCORED 10 GOALS.

SVEN-GÖRAN ERIKSSON GAVE *COLE* HIS *ENGLAND* DEBUT. WHICH MANAGER GAVE A FIRST *ENGLAND* CAP TO THE FOLLOWING PLAYERS?

1 *ALVIN MARTIN:* MAY, 1981, *ENGLAND* 0 *BRAZIL* 1

2 *TONY COTTEE:* SEPTEMBER, 1986, *SWEDEN* 1 *ENGLAND* 0

3 *AARON CRESSWELL:* NOVEMBER, 2016, *ENGLAND* 2 *SPAIN* 2

4 *RIO FERDINAND:* NOVEMBER, 1997, *ENGLAND* 2 *CAMEROON* 0

5 *CARLTON COLE:* FEBRUARY, 2009, *SPAIN* 2 *ENGLAND* 0

6 *BOBBY MOORE:* MAY, 1962, *PERU* 0 *ENGLAND* 4

7 *PHIL PARKES:* APRIL, 1974, *PORTUGAL* 0 *ENGLAND* 0

8 *STUART PEARSON:* MAY, 1976, *WALES* 0 *ENGLAND* 1

9 *IAN WRIGHT:* FEBRUARY, 1991, *ENGLAND* 2 *CAMEROON* 0

10 *FRANK LAMPARD:* OCTOBER, 1999, *ENGLAND* 2 *BELGIUM* 1

11 *ROB LEE:* OCTOBER, 1994, *ENGLAND* 1 *ROMANIA* 1

12 *DAVID UNSWORTH:* JUNE, 1995, *ENGLAND* 2 *JAPAN* 1

13 *PAUL GODDARD:* JUNE, 1982, *ICELAND* 1 *ENGLAND* 1

14 *MICHAEL CARRICK:* MAY, 2001, *ENGLAND* 4 *MEXICO* 0

15 *MARTIN PETERS:* MAY, 1966, *ENGLAND* 2 *YUGOSLAVIA* 0

SAMBA SOCCER

ARGENTINA INTERNATIONAL **CARLOS TEVEZ** SPENT TWO SEASONS IN BRAZIL WITH **CORINTHIANS**, DURING WHICH TIME HE CAPTAINED THE SQUAD TO THE 2005 CAMPEONATO BRASILEIRO, WAS NAMED THE LEAGUE'S BEST PLAYER BY THE BRAZILIAN FOOTBALL CONFEDERATION -- THE FIRST NON-BRAZILIAN PLAYER TO WIN THE AWARD SINCE 1976 -- AND WON HIS THIRD SOUTH AMERICAN FOOTBALLER OF THE YEAR AWARD.

NAME THESE OTHER **HAMMERS** WHO PLAYED CLUB FOOTBALL IN BRAZIL:

1 STRIKER WHO ARRIVED AT **WEST HAM** ON LOAN IN 2013 HAVING WON HONOURS IN HIS NATIVE BRAZIL WITH **BOTAFOGO** AND **CRUZEIRO** BUT -- HAVING FAILED TO GET A GAME -- RETURNED HOME TO WIN HONOURS WITH **CHAPECOENSE** AND **FORTALEZA**.

2 A 2011 COPA LIBERTADORES AND 2012 RECOPA SUDAMERICANA WINNER WITH **SANTOS**, MIDFIELDER WHO WON HONOURS WITH **LAZIO**. A 2016 OLYMPIC GOLD MEDAL WINNER WITH **BRAZIL**, HE SPENT THREE YEARS WITH **WEST HAM** -- SOME OF WHICH WERE ON LOAN AT **PORTO** -- BEFORE RETURNING TO **LAZIO** IN 2021.

3 HAVING WON HONOURS IN HIS HOMELAND WITH **PAULISTA**, HIS TRAVELS TOOK HIM TO CLUBS IN SPAIN, FRANCE -- HE WON A LEAGUE TITLE WITH **PARIS SAINT-GERMAIN** -- AND QATAR, BEFORE AN UNSUCCESSFUL SPELL WITH **WEST HAM** IN 2015. HE RETURNED TO BRAZIL AND WON FURTHER HONOURS WITH **VASCO DA GAMA** AND **SÃO PAULO**.

4 **ARGENTINA** INTERNATIONAL WHOSE CLUBS INCLUDED **CORINTHIANS**, **WEST HAM**, **LIVERPOOL** AND **BARCELONA**.

5 YOUNG MIDFIELD SCHEMER WHO JOINED **THE HAMMERS** FROM **FLAMENGO** AS A YOUNG TEEN AND WAS IN EXCEPTIONAL FORM AS THE **U23** TEAM WERE CROWNED CHAMPIONS OF THE PREMIER LEAGUE 2 DIVISION 2 FOR THE 2019/20 SEASON.

6 **COLOMBIA** LEFT-BACK WHO PLAYED A HANDFUL OF GAMES ON LOAN WITH **THE HAMMERS** IN 2014, HE PLAYED FOR A NUMBER OF CLUBS IN ITALY AND BRAZIL.

7   ARGENTINE STRIKER WHO SPENT THE 2016-17 SEASON ON LOAN WITH **WEST HAM**, HE HAS PLAYED FOR CLUBS IN ARGENTINA, URUGUAY, BRAZIL AND SPAIN.

8   **PARAGUAY** CENTRE-BACK WHO JOINED **THE HAMMERS** IN 2018 AFTER WINNING TITLES WITH **CORINTHIANS**, HE SIGNED FOR **DYNAMO MOSCOW** IN THE SUMMER OF 2021.

9   ARGENTINE FORWARD WHOSE ENGLISH CLUBS INCLUDE **BIRMINGHAM CITY**, **QUEENS PARK RANGERS** AND WATFORD, HE JOINED WEST HAM FROM VÉLEZ SARSFIELD IN 2016 AND HAS SUBSEQUENTLY PLAYED IN ITALY, THE UAE AND BRAZIL.

10   **BRAZIL** STRIKER WHO PLAYED IN HIS HOMELAND AND FRANCE BEFORE JOINING **WEST HAM** IN EARLY 2010, SCORING THREE MINUTES AFTER COMING ON AS A SUB IN HIS DEBUT.

WELL, I NEVER ...

IN 2017, THE THREE-PART TV DRAMA SERIES *"TINA AND BOBBY"* WAS CENTRED AROUND THE STORY OF *BOBBY MOORE* AND HIS WIFE *TINA.*

1 WHICH FORMER *WEST HAM* RIGHT-BACK -- WHOSE CLUBS INCLUDE *PRESTON, DERBY COUNTY, BURNLEY* AND *BOLTON WANDERERS* -- WAS CAPPED BY *JAMAICA* IN 2009 EVEN THOUGH HE WAS ACTUALLY INELIGIBLE TO PLAY FOR THAT COUNTRY?

2 WHICH SUBSEQUENT *WEST HAM* PLAYER SCORED EIGHT GOALS AT THE 2004 OLYMPICS?

3 WHICH FORMER *WEST HAM* STRIKER APPEARED IN THE 2018 *PIERCE BROSNAN* ACTION FILM *"FINAL SCORE"?*

4 NAME THE *WEST HAM* WINGER, SON OF A PASTOR, WHOSE PARENTS WERE KILLED IN RELIGIOUS UNREST IN NIGERIA WHEN RIOTERS INVADED THEIR HOME, WHILE THE 11-YEAR-OLD WAS PLAYING FOOTBALL IN THE STREET. AFTER BEING HIDDEN BY FRIENDS, HIS RELATIVES PAID FOR HIM TO TRAVEL TO THE UK TO CLAIM ASYLUM, WHERE HE WAS SUBSEQUENTLY FOSTERED.

5 WHICH FORMER *WEST HAM* GOALKEEPER'S "MASTERPIECE" ART INSTALLATION -- A GRAFFITI-DAUBED HORSE BOX WITH MATTRESSES AND A SEX DOLL STRAPPED TO IT -- IN THE GARDEN OF HIS DERBYSHIRE HOME, DREW THE IRE OF HIS NEIGHBOURS ?

6 WHICH FORMER *HAMMER* WAS REFUSED A PROFESSIONAL BOXING LICENCE BY THE BRITISH BOXING BOARD OF CONTROL IN 2018?

7 WHICH *WEST HAM* MANAGER PLAYED IN A ROCK BAND CALLED *RAWBAU?*

8 AHEAD OF THE 1980 FA CUP FINAL, WHICH PUNK BAND RELEASED A VERSION OF *"I'M FOREVER BLOWING BUBBLES"*?

9 A STATUE ERECTED NEAR *THE BOLEYN GROUND*, HONOURING *WEST HAM'S* 1966 WORLD CUP HEROES, ALSO INCLUDES WHICH *EVERTON* PLAYER?

10 WHICH FORMER *WEST HAM* AND *SCOTLAND* GOALKEEPER, AFTER EMIGRATING TO AUSTRALIA, RAN A DIVING FIRM FOR A NUMBER OF YEARS BUT ABANDONED THE BUSINESS AFTER A COLLEAGUE WAS ATTACKED BY A SHARK?

THE CRYSTAL METHOD

MAROUANE CHAMAKH ESTABLISHED HIS GOALSCORING PROWESS AT **BORDEAUX**, HELPING THE CLUB TO WIN A LEAGUE AND CUP DOUBLE AND WINNING THE CLUB'S 2010 PLAYER OF THE YEAR AWARD. MOVING ON TO **ARSENAL**, HE BECAME THE FIRST PLAYER TO SCORE IN SIX CONSECUTIVE EUROPEAN CHAMPIONS LEAGUE GAMES. FOLLOWING A SHORT LOAN SPELL WITH **WEST HAM**, HE SPENT THREE SEASONS AT **CRYSTAL PALACE**, BEFORE A BRIEF SPELL AT **CARDIFF CITY**. HE RETIRED IN 2019 HAVING NOT PLAYED FOR ALMOST TWO AND A HALF YEARS.

NAME THESE OTHER **HAMMERS** WHO PLAYED FOR **CRYSTAL PALACE**:

1 STRIKER, MOST NOTABLY WITH **WEST HAM**, **SOUTHAMPTON**, **CRYSTAL PALACE** AND **QUEENS PARK RANGERS**, CAPPED 59 TIMES BY **NORTHERN IRELAND**. AS A MANAGER, HE STEERED **PALACE** TO PROMOTION TO THE PREMIER LEAGUE IN 2003.

2 MIDFIELDER WHO JOINED **WEST HAM** IN 2003 AFTER MAKING 257 APPEARANCES IN HIS FIVE YEARS AT **PALACE**. HE WENT ON TO PLAY IN AN FA CUP FINAL FOR **PORTSMOUTH**, PLAY FOR **READING**, **BIRMINGHAM CITY** AND **NOTTS COUNTY** AND MANAGE **COLCHESTER UNITED**.

3 A PROMOTION WINNER WITH **THE HAMMERS** IN 2013, CENTRE-BACK WHO JOINED **PALACE** IN A £10 MILLION DEAL IN 2016.

4 STRIKER WHO HAD TWO SPELLS WITH **CRYSTAL PALACE** EITHER SIDE OF HIS FIVE YEARS WITH **THE HAMMERS**, DURING WHICH TIME HE WON THE 1964 FA CUP. AN **ENGLAND** INTERNATIONAL, HE EMIGRATED TO SOUTH AFRICA IN 1969.

5 HARDMAN DEFENDER WHO HAD TWO SPELLS EACH WITH **MILLWALL** AND **SPURS**, HE JOINED WEST HAM FROM LIVERPOOL IN 1998. TWO SEASONS LATER, HE MADE THE MOVE TO **CRYSTAL PALACE**.

6 STRIKER WHOSE CAREER TOOK HIM FROM **LEICESTER CITY** TO **DERBY COUNTY** AND **NEWCASTLE UNITED**, BEFORE SIGNING TO **WEST HAM** IN 1997. FOLLOWING LOAN SPELLS AT **CHARLTON** AND **PALACE**, HE JOINED **BRIGHTON & HOVE ALBION** IN 2002.

"HE'S HARDER THAN JAAP STAM ..."

WHILE PLAYING FOR *WEST HAM, PABLO ZABALETA* -- WHO SIGNED FROM *MANCHESTER CITY* ON A FREE TRANSFER IN 2017 -- BECAME THE FIRST ARGENTINE, AND ONLY THE THIRD SOUTH AMERICAN, TO MAKE 300 PREMIER LEAGUE APPEARANCES.

1 *ZABALETA* WON MULTIPLE HONOURS WITH *MANCHESTER CITY* -- BUT WITH WHICH CLUB DID HE WIN THE 2006 COPA DEL REY?

2 WHICH *ARGENTINA* INTERNATIONAL, NICKNAMED *"LA JOYA"* -- *"THE JEWEL"* -- JOINED *WEST HAM* ON LOAN IN 2015, THE MOVE BECOMING PERMANENT THE FOLLOWING YEAR?

3 NAME THE ARGENTINE RIGHT-BACK WHO JOINED *THE HAMMERS* ON LOAN, TAKING THE NUMBER 2 SHIRT FROM THE DEPARTED *TOMÁŠ ŘEPKA*, BEFORE PLAYING IN THE 2006 FA CUP FINAL.

4 NAME THE ARGENTINE FULL-BACK WHO, HAVING PLAYED A DECADE IN ENGLAND WITH *IPSWICH TOWN* AND *SPURS*, TORE HIS HAMSTRING ON HIS *WEST HAM* DEBUT IN 2004 AND THEN INSISTED ON THE CLUB TEARING UP HIS CONTRACT, A GESTURE MANAGER *ALAN PARDEW* DEEMED ONE OF THE MOST HONEST THINGS HE HAD EVER KNOWN A FOOTBALLER TO DO.

5 NAME ONE OF THE TWO TEAMS IN ARGENTINA MANAGED BY SUBSEQUENT *WEST HAM* BOSS *MANUEL PELLEGRINI.*

6 WHO WAS THE ARGENTINE STRIKER SIGNED ON LOAN TO *WEST HAM* FROM URUGUAY'S *DEPORTIVO MALDONADO* IN 2016?

7 ON THE FINAL DAY OF THE 2006-07 SEASON, *ARGENTINA* SUPERSTAR *CARLOS TEVEZ* SCORED THE ONLY GOAL OF THE GAME TO GIVE *THE HAMMERS* THE VICTORY THAT KEPT THEM IN THE PREMIER LEAGUE -- WHO WERE THE OPPONENTS?

8 WHAT DOES THE NICKNAME OF *ARGENTINA* GREAT *JAVIER MASCHERANO* -- *"EL JEFECITO"* -- MEAN IN ENGLISH?

THE ONES THAT GOT AWAY

RODNEY MARSH, THE MAVERICK ENGLAND INTERNATIONAL WHO WON HONOURS WITH QUEENS PARK RANGERS, MANCHESTER CITY, TAMPA BAY ROWDIES AND CAROLINA LIGHTNIN', PLAYED YOUTH FOOTBALL FOR WEST HAM BUT WAS RELEASED FROM THE ACADEMY TO MAKE ROOM FOR GEOFF HURST. MARSH WAS PICKED UP BY FULHAM AND MADE HIS PROFESSIONAL DEBUT FOR "THE COTTAGERS" AT 18.

IDENTIFY THESE OTHER WEST HAM YOUTH TEAM MEMBERS WHO NEVER PLAYED FOR THE FIRST TEAM:

1 CENTRE-BACK WHO PLAYED FOR TOTTENHAM HOTSPUR, ARSENAL, PORTSMOUTH, NOTTS COUNTY AND NEWCASTLE UNITED, CAPPED 73 TIMES BY ENGLAND.

2 CENTRE-BACK WHO WON NUMEROUS HONOURS WITH CHELSEA, INCLUDING FIVE LEAGUE TITLES, THE UEFA CHAMPIONS LEAGUE AND EUROPA LEAGUE, CAPPED 78 TIMES BY ENGLAND.

3 CAPPED EIGHT TIMES BY ENGLAND, VERSATILE PLAYER WHO WON THE 2007 PREMIER LEAGUE WITH MANCHESTER UNITED, MOVED ON TO WEST BROMWICH ALBION, SUNDERLAND AND FULHAM, THEN PLAYED IN THE 2015 FA CUP FINAL WITH ASTON VILLA BEFORE JOINING CARDIFF CITY.

4 "SOCCER AM" TV PERSONALITY WHOSE CLUBS INCLUDED PETERBOROUGH UNITED, WIGAN ATHLETIC, FULHAM, HULL CITY, IPSWICH TOWN AND MILTON KEYNES DONS.

5 TRINIDAD AND TOBAGO DEFENDER WHO SPENT EIGHT SEASONS AT ASTON VILLA AND FOUR AT BOLTON WANDERERS, HE WAS KILLED IN A CAR CRASH IN CHESHIRE IN 2018.

6 CAPPED 11 TIMES BY WALES, FORWARD WHO WON TWO PROMOTIONS WITH SOUTHEND UNITED AND PLAYED WITH WOLVERHAMPTON WANDERERS AND COVENTRY CITY.

7 DEFENDER WHO CAPTAINED CRYSTAL PALACE AND WON THE CHAMPIONSHIP WITH NEWCASTLE IN 2010 AND QPR IN 2011.

HAMMER RAMS!

THE FIRST AMERICAN TO PLAY IN THE ENGLISH PREMIER LEAGUE, *JOHN HARKES* JOINED *SHEFFIELD WEDNESDAY* IN 1990. HE WAS ON THE LOSING SIDE IN AN FA CUP FINAL AND THE WINNING SIDE IN A LEAGUE CUP FINAL, BEFORE SIGNING FOR *DERBY COUNTY*. WHILE WAITING FOR THE LAUNCH OF MAJOR LEAGUE SOCCER, HE PLAYED ON LOAN FOR *WEST HAM*, THEN RETURNED STATESIDE TO PLAY FOR *D.C. UNITED*, *NEW ENGLAND REVOLUTION* AND *COLUMBUS CREW*. *HARKES* WON A TOTAL OF 90 *USA* CAPS AND WAS A STAR OF THE 1990 AND 1994 WORLD CUPS. ALTHOUGH HE WAS NATIONAL TEAM CAPTAIN, HE WAS CONTROVERSIALLY DROPPED FROM THE 1998 SQUAD AMID RUMOURS OF PERSONAL CONFLICTS BEHIND THE SCENES.

NAME THESE OTHERS WHO PLAYED FOR *DERBY* AND *WEST HAM*:

1 *COSTA RICA* STRIKER WHOSE CLUBS INCLUDED *DERBY*, *WEST HAM* AND *MANCHESTER CITY*, AS WELL AS TEAMS IN SPAIN, QATAR, ARGENTINA, JAPAN AND THE USA.

2 *CROATIA* DEFENDER WHO GAINED PROMOTION WITH *"THE RAMS"* IN 1996, AND SPENT TWO SEASONS AT *WEST HAM* BEFORE RETURNING TO BOYHOOD CLUB *HAJDUK SPLIT* IN 2001.

3 RIGHT-BACK WHO BEGAN HIS CAREER AT *MANCHESTER CITY* BEFORE PLAYING FOR *PRESTON NORTH END*, *WEST HAM*, *DERBY COUNTY*, *OLYMPIQUE DE MARSEILLE*, *BURNLEY*, *BOLTON WANDERERS*, SPENDING FOUR YEARS IN AMERICAN SOCCER AND THEN SIGNING FOR *WEST BROM* IN 2018.

4 GOALKEEPER WHOSE LENGTHY LIST OF CLUBS INCLUDES *WEST HAM*, *DERBY COUNTY*, *HULL CITY*, *IPSWICH TOWN*, *CARDIFF CITY*, *SHEFFIELD WEDNESDAY*, *MILLWALL* AND *BURTON ALBION*. HE HAS WORN THE NUMBER 43 SHIRT IN MEMORY OF HIS MENTOR AND COACH, THE LATE *LES SEALEY*.

5 SECOND DIVISION WINNER WITH *CRYSTAL PALACE* IN 1979, STRIKER WHO PLAYED FOR *DERBY COUNTY*, *WEST HAM* AND *SUNDERLAND* DURING THE 1980S.

6 CAPPED 21 TIMES BY *ENGLAND*, MIDFIELDER WHO PLAYED FOR *CHARLTON ATHLETIC*, *NEWCASTLE UNITED*, *DERBY*, *WEST HAM*, *OLDHAM ATHLETIC* AND *WYCOMBE WANDERERS*.

7 *CHARLTON ATHLETIC'S* ALL-TIME LEADING GOALSCORER, HE HAD TWO SPELLS AT THE CLUB, EITHER SIDE OF SPELLS IN THE LATE 1970S WITH *DERBY COUNTY* AND *WEST HAM*.

8 *WEST HAM* ACADEMY GRADUATE CENTRE-BACK WHO HAD A BRIEF LOAN SPELL AT *DERBY COUNTY* EARLY IN HIS CAREER. HE PLAYED 243 GAMES IN HIS NINE SEASONS WITH *THE HAMMERS* BEFORE JOINING *CRYSTAL PALACE* IN 2016.

9 DEFENDER WHO BROKE HIS LEG IN TWO PLACES DURING HIS SPELL AT *SHEFFIELD UNITED*, ONLY TO HAVE THE INJURY RE-INFLICTED BY A TRAINING-GROUND TACKLE BY *JULIAN DICKS* WITHIN WEEKS OF JOINING *WEST HAM* IN 1993. HE PLAYED BRIEFLY ON LOAN AT *DERBY COUNTY* BEFORE RETIRING TO STUDY PHYSIOTHERAPY.

IRONS DOWN UNDER

A PROLIFIC GOALSCORER CAPPED SEVEN TIMES BY **SCOTLAND**, **TED MACDOUGALL'S** CLUBS INCLUDED **MANCHESTER UNITED**, **WEST HAM**, **NORWICH CITY**, **SOUTHAMPTON** AND TWO SPELLS WITH **BOURNEMOUTH** -- FOR WHOM HE ONCE SCORED 9 GOALS IN AN 11-0 WIN OVER **MARGATE** IN 1971. IN THE EARLY 1980S HE PLIED HIS TRADE IN AUSTRALIA, PLAYING FOR **FLOREAT ATHENA** IN PERTH AND SYDNEY SIDE **ST GEORGE-BUDAPEST**.

IDENTIFY THESE **WEST HAM** PLAYERS WITH LINKS TO AUSTRALIA:

1 HAVING WON HONOURS WITH **ENGLAND**, **WEST HAM** AND **SPURS**, DURING HIS TIME WITH **NORWICH CITY** IN THE LATE 1970S HE GUESTED WITH AUSSIE SIDE **FRANKSTON CITY**.

2 CAPPED 96 TIMES BY **AUSTRALIA**, DURING HIS 15 YEARS IN ENGLAND BETWEEN 1995 AND 2010, HE PLAYED FOR **MILLWALL**, **BLACKBURN ROVERS**, **EVERTON** AND CAPTAINED **WEST HAM**, BEFORE PLAYING IN TURKEY, THE MIDDLE EAST AND JAPAN.

3 HIS £65,000 FEE FROM **KILMARNOCK** IN 1967 WAS A WORLD RECORD FOR A GOALKEEPER. **THE HAMMERS** WERE REWARDED WITH 276 APPEARANCES IN HIS 13 YEARS AT THE **BOLEYN GROUND**. HE MOVED TO AUSTRALIA IN 1982 TO PLAY FOR **ADELAIDE CITY**.

4 AUSTRALIAN STRIKER WHO MADE HIS DEBUT FOR **WEST HAM** AT THE AGE OF 18 IN 2012 -- WHILE IN THE MIDST OF CHEMOTHERAPY TREATMENT. FOLLOWING HIS PASSING IN 2014, THE CLUB RETIRED HIS NUMBER 38 SHIRT.

5 **WEST ADELAIDE** WINGER SPOTTED AND SIGNED BY **HARRY REDKNAPP** FOLLOWING THE 1995 AUSTRALIAN TOUR, HE SPENT FIVE SEASONS WITH **WEST HAM** AND SEVEN WITH **BIRMINGHAM CITY**.

6 HAVING IMPRESSED AT THE 2000 OLYMPICS, **AUSTRALIA** CENTRE-BACK WHO SPENT TWO SEASONS WITH **WEST HAM**, WON A FIRST DIVISION TITLE WITH **PORTSMOUTH** AND PLAYED FOR **LEEDS UNITED** BEFORE RETURNING TO AUSTRALIA IN 2007.

7 CAPPED 44 TIMES, HE WAS THE FIRST AUSSIE TO WIN A PREMIER LEAGUE TITLE, WITH *BLACKBURN ROVERS* IN 1995, BEFORE PLAYING FOR *WEST HAM*, *SOUTHAMPTON* AND *WOLVES*.

8 AUSTRALIA-BORN PRODUCT OF THE *WEST HAM* YOUTH SYSTEM, HE WENT ON TO PLAY FOR *LEYTON ORIENT*, *COLCHESTER UNITED* AND *HULL CITY*, CLUBS IN THE USA AND AUSTRALIA AND WAS APPOINTED HEAD COACH OF *PERTH GLORY* IN 2020.

HIS NAME IS RIO

RIO FERDINAND WAS NAMED IN FOUR CONSECUTIVE **ENGLAND** WORLD CUP SQUADS, ALTHOUGH HE DIDN'T PLAY IN 1998 AND MISSED THE 2010 TOURNAMENT THROUGH INJURY. FOR A VARIETY OF REASONS, HE NEVER REPRESENTED HIS COUNTRY IN A EUROPEAN CHAMPIONSHIP. HE WAS OMITTED FROM THE 2000 SQUAD ... MISSED OUT IN 2004 DUE TO A BAN FOR MISSING A DRUGS TEST ... **ENGLAND** FAILED TO QUALIFY FOR EURO 2008 ... AND HE WAS LEFT OUT OF THE 2012 SQUAD AMID SPECULATION THAT HIS ABSENCE WAS TO AVOID POTENTIAL CONFLICT WITH **JOHN TERRY**, WHO WAS DUE TO STAND TRIAL OVER A CHARGE HE RACIALLY ABUSED **RIO'S** BROTHER **ANTON. TERRY** WAS ACQUITTED.

1 NAME THE THREE ERSTWHILE **WEST HAM** PLAYERS WHO APPEARED IN THREE WORLD CUP TOURNAMENTS FOR **ENGLAND.**

2 **FERDINAND** PLAYED FOR **ENGLAND** IN 15 CONSECUTIVE YEARS, A RECORD HE SHARES WITH WHICH **ARSENAL** GOALKEEPER?

3 AT THE AGE OF 31 YEARS AND 260 DAYS IN 1980, WHICH **WEST HAM** PLAYER BECAME **ENGLAND'S** OLDEST GOALSCORER AT THE EUROPEAN CHAMPIONSHIP FINALS?

4 WHICH **WEST HAM** PLAYER WAS **ENGLAND'S** YOUNGEST CAPTAIN, AGED 22 YEARS AND 47 DAYS?

5 WHICH **WEST HAM** PLAYER BECAME THE FIRST **ENGLAND** GOALKEEPER TO BE SENT OFF?

6 WHICH FORMER **WEST HAM** DEFENDER IS AMONG THE GROUP OF **ENGLAND** PLAYERS WHO WENT ON TO MANAGE **ENGLAND**?

7 WHICH FATHER AND SON WERE BOTH **WEST HAM** PLAYERS WHO PLAYED FOR **ENGLAND**?

8 NAME THE SEVEN MANAGERS UNDER WHOM **RIO FERDINAND** PLAYED FOR **ENGLAND** BETWEEN 1997 AND 2011.

GETTING SHIRTY!

IN 1989, WITH THE £1 MILLION DEAL AGREED THAT WOULD TAKE HIM FROM *WEST HAM* TO *MANCHESTER UNITED*, *PAUL INCE* WENT ON HOLIDAY. BEFORE HE LEFT, HE POSED IN A *UNITED* SHIRT, THE PHOTO TO BE RELEASED TO THE MEDIA WHEN THE SIGNING WAS ANNOUNCED. IT LEAKED EARLY, INVITING THE WRATH AND SCORN OF THE CLARET AND BLUE ARMY!

AT WHICH CLUBS DID *INCE* PLAY UNDER THE FOLLOWING MANAGERS?

1   *TERRY VENABLES*

2   *GLENN HODDLE*

3   *ROY HODGSON*

4   *GÉRARD HOULLIER*

5   *DENNIS WISE*

6   *JOHN LYALL*

7   *DAVE JONES*

8   *STEVE MCLAREN*

9   *ROY EVANS*

10   *LUIS SUÁREZ*

¡VIVA ESPAÑA!

IN 2017, **PABLO FORNALS** PAID HIS OWN €12 MILLION BUYOUT CLAUSE TO LEAVE **MÁLAGA** FOR **VILLARREAL**. TWO YEARS LATER, THE £24 MILLION THAT **WEST HAM** PAID TO BRING HIM TO LONDON WAS THE SECOND MOST EXPENSIVE TRANSFER FEE OUTLAY IN CLUB HISTORY.

FROM WHICH SPANISH CLUB DID THE FOLLOWING JOIN **WEST HAM**?

1 **ALEX SONG** (2014)

2 **GUILLERMO FRANCO** (2009)

3 **ROBERTO** (2019)

4 **YOSSI BENAYOUN** (2005)

5 **ADRIÁN** (2013)

6 **KEPA BLANCO** (2007)

7 **LIONEL SCALONI** (2006)

8 **SOFIANE FEGHOULI** (2016)

9 **ÁLVARO ARBELOA** (2016)

10 **FLORIN RĂDUCIOIU** (1996)

THE EARLY BATH

CAMEROON'S RIGOBERT SONG AND **ZINEDINE ZIDANE** OF **FRANCE** ARE THE ONLY TWO PLAYERS TO HAVE BEEN SENT OFF IN TWO DIFFERENT WORLD CUPS. **SONG** WAS DISMISSED AGAINST **BRAZIL** IN 1994 AND AGAINST **CHILE** IN 1998. HE ALSO HOLDS THE RECORD AS THE YOUNGEST PLAYER EVER TO BE SENT OFF IN A WORLD CUP TOURNAMENT, AGED 17! **RIGOBERT'S** NEPHEW, **ALEX SONG**, WAS RED-CARDED PLAYING FOR **CAMEROON** AGAINST **CROATIA** IN 2014.

1 WHICH SUBSEQUENT **HAMMER** WAS SENT OFF IN THE 2013 FA CUP FINAL PLAYING AGAINST **WIGAN ATHLETIC**?

2 WHICH **CHELSEA** PLAYER, WHO HAD SPENT THE PREVIOUS SEASON ON LOAN AT **WEST HAM**, RECEIVED TWO YELLOW CARDS IN THE 2017 FA CUP FINAL?

3 WHICH **WEST HAM** PLAYER WAS DEEMED "STUPID" BY **DAVID MOYES** AFTER RECEIVING HIS MARCHING ORDERS AGAINST **SOUTHAMPTON** IN A SEPTEMBER, 2021 GAME?

4 WHICH MIDFIELDER, WHILE AT **LEEDS UNITED**, FOLLOWED THE STAMP ON **VALENCIA'S JUAN SANCHEZ** IN THE CHAMPIONS LEAGUE SEMI-FINAL THAT EARNED HIM A THREE-GAME BAN WITH A RASH TACKLE AND STAMP ON THE HEAD OF **MÁLAGA** MIDFIELDER **GERARDO** THAT SAW HIM BANNED FOR SIX GAMES? HE SUBSEQUENTLY EARNED HIMSELF A SIX-GAME BAN FOR FIGHTING WITH A TEAMMATE WHILE PLAYING FOR **NEWCASTLE UNITED**.

5 WHICH WELSH STRIKER AVERAGED ONE RED CARD EVERY 26 GAMES IN THE PREMIER LEAGUE, FROM 1995 TO 2001?

6 IN 2011, WHICH STRIKER'S OVER-EXUBERANT CELEBRATION OF HIS GOAL AT **EVERTON**, JUMPING INTO THE CROWD TO CELEBRATE HIS LATE GOAL, EARNED HIM A SECOND YELLOW?

7 WHICH GOALKEEPER WAS SENT OFF FOUR TIMES DURING HIS TIME AT **BOLTON WANDERERS** AND RACKED UP 25 YELLOW CARDS FOR CLUB AND COUNTRY DURING HIS CAREER?

8 WHICH MIDFIELDER'S 2021 RED CARD WAS OVERTURNED ON APPEAL AFTER **FULHAM'S ALEKSANDAR MITROVIĆ** TESTIFIED THAT THE ELBOW THAT CAUGHT HIM WAS COMPLETELY ACCIDENTAL?

TAKING EARLY RETIREMENT

HAVING PLAYED HIS LAST GAME AT THE AGE OF 28, A DISILLUSIONED **DAVID BENTLEY** RETIRED FROM FOOTBALL AT THE AGE OF 29. THE **ENGLAND** INTERNATIONAL WINGER MOVED WITH HIS FAMILY TO MARBELLA TO RUN HIS BAR AND RESTAURANT.

FOR WHICH TEAM DID HE PLAY UNDER THESE MANAGERS?

1 *ARSÈNE WENGER*

2 *MIODRAG BOŽOVIĆ*

3 *GARY BOWYER*

4 *SAM ALLARDYCE*

5 *ALEX MCLEISH*

6 *MICHAEL APPLETON*

7 *HARRY REDKNAPP*

8 *MARK HUGHES*

9 *NIGEL WORTHINGTON*

10 *JUANDE RAMOS*

OLD GLORY!

HAVING MANAGED **PLYMOUTH ARGYLE** FOR THREE SEASONS, 45-YEAR-OLD **PETER SHILTON** ANNOUNCED THAT HE WOULD RESUME HIS PLAYING CAREER, INTENT ON REACHING HIS GOAL OF 1,000 CAREER FOOTBALL LEAGUE MATCHES. HE JOINED **WIMBLEDON**, BUT FAILED TO MAKE AN APPEARANCE. HE JOINED **BOLTON WANDERERS**, WHERE HE ADDED ONE LEAGUE GAME TO HIS TALLY BEFORE MOVING ON TO **COVENTRY CITY**. WHEN HE FAILED TO FIND A GAME WITH **THE SKY BLUES**, HE TRIED HIS LUCK WITH A SPELL AT **WEST HAM**, ONCE MORE FAILING TO MAKE AN APPEARANCE. FINALLY, AFTER DROPPING DOWN TO THE FOURTH TIER WITH **LEYTON ORIENT**, HIS NINE APPEARANCES TOOK HIS TOTAL TO 1,005 LEAGUE GAMES ... AND HIS OVERALL CAREER RECORD TO 1,390 GAMES!

IDENTIFY THESE **WEST HAM** KEEPERS BY THE TEAMS THEY PLAYED FOR:

1 WEST HAM 2004 : **BANÍK OSTRAVA, NEWCASTLE UNITED, SHEFFIELD WEDNESDAY, BRESCIA, COSENZA, PORTSMOUTH, BEIRA-MAR**

2 WEST HAM 2001-2004 : **WATFORD, LIVERPOOL, ASTON VILLA, MANCHESTER CITY, PORTSMOUTH, BRISTOL CITY, AFC BOURNEMOUTH, ÍBV VESTMANNAEYJA, KERALA BLASTERS**

3 WEST HAM 1979-1990 : **WALSALL, QUEENS PARK RANGERS, IPSWICH TOWN**

4 WEST HAM (LOAN) 2017-2018 : **SHREWSBURY TOWN, MANCHESTER CITY, TRANMERE ROVERS** (LOAN), **BLACKPOOL** (LOAN), **BIRMINGHAM CITY** (LOAN), **TORINO** (LOAN), **BURNLEY, TOTTENHAM HOTSPUR, CELTIC**

5 WEST HAM 2013-2019 : **BETIS C, BETIS B, ALCALÁ** (LOAN), **UTRERA** (LOAN), **BETIS, LIVERPOOL**

6   **WEST HAM** 2012-2015 : *MP, VPS, BOLTON WANDERERS, WIGAN ATHLETIC, ATK*

7   **WEST HAM** 1973-1979 : *LEYTON ORIENT, ASTON VILLA, LEEDS UNITED, LUTON TOWN* (LOAN), *SHEFFIELD UNITED* (LOAN), *CARLISLE UNITED*

8   **WEST HAM** 1962-1968 : *ARSENAL, LUTON TOWN, DETROIT COUGARS, MILLWALL, PORTSMOUTH*

9   **WEST HAM** 1994-1996, 1996-2001 : *COVENTRY CITY, LUTON TOWN, PLYMOUTH ARGYLE* (LOAN), *MANCHESTER UNITED, ASTON VILLA, BIRMINGHAM CITY, BLACKPOOL, LEYTON ORIENT, BURY* (LOAN)

10   **WEST HAM** 2005-2007 : *HULL CITY, WIGAN ATHLETIC, MANCHESTER UNITED, RANGERS, DERBY COUNTY, ODENSE BK, OFI CRETE, OLYMPIACOS, NOTTS COUNTY, LINFIELD, FC MINDWELL, DUNGANNON SWIFTS*

11   **WEST HAM** 2006-2012 : *NORWICH CITY, QUEENS PARK RANGERS, LEEDS UNITED, HUDDERSFIELD TOWN, CHELSEA*

12   WEST HAM (LOAN) 2011: *OSASUNA B, OSASUNA, CARTAGONOVA* (LOAN), *SABADELL, CELTA, EIBAR* (LOAN), *RECREATIVO* (LOAN), *ALBACETE* (LOAN), *ARSENAL, WATFORD*

COTTAGERS AND HAMMERS

WEMBLEY STADIUM HAD NOT ONLY SEEN **ENGLAND** CAPTAIN **BOBBY MOORE** LIFT THE WORLD CUP, HE HAD LED **WEST HAM** TO WEMBLEY TRIUMPH IN THE 1964 FA CUP FINAL AND THE 1965 EUROPEAN CUP WINNERS' CUP FINAL. A YEAR AFTER LEAVING **THE HAMMERS** FOR **FULHAM**, HIS FINAL APPEARANCE AT THE VENERATED HOME OF FOOTBALL ENDED IN DISAPPOINTMENT, HIS NEW TEAM GOING DOWN 2-0 TO HIS OLD TEAM IN THE 1975 FA CUP FINAL.

IDENTIFY THESE OTHERS WHO PLAYED FOR **WEST HAM** AND **FULHAM**:

1 STRIKER WHO HAD THREE SEPARATE SPELLS WITH **FULHAM**, PLAYED FOR **QPR** IN THE 1986 LEAGUE CUP FINAL, SPENT FOUR SEASONS AT **WEST HAM**, JOINED **BRISTOL CITY** AND LATER MANAGED A NUMBER OF TEAMS, INCLUDING **TORQUAY UNITED** TWICE.

2 CAPPED TWICE BY **ENGLAND** DURING A 21-YEAR PLAYING CAREER, LEFT-BACK WHOSE CLUBS INCLUDED **CHARLTON ATHLETIC, SPURS, WEST HAM, FULHAM, LIVERPOOL, NOTTINGHAM FOREST, QUEENS PARK RANGERS** AND **LEICESTER CITY**.

3 **REPUBLIC OF IRELAND** MIDFIELDER WHO, HAVING FAILED TO BREAK THROUGH AT **WEST HAM**, ESTABLISHED HIS REPUTATION AT **FULHAM**, WON A LEAGUE CUP WITH **OXFORD UNITED**, TWO LEAGUE TITLES AND TWO FA CUPS WITH **LIVERPOOL** AND THE 1994 LEAGUE CUP WITH **ASTON VILLA**.

4 **ENGLAND** STRIKER WHO FOLLOWED SUCCESSIVE PROMOTIONS WITH **BRIGHTON & HOVE ALBION** AND A BRIEF SPELL WITH **SPURS** WITH PROMOTION AT **WEST HAM**, THE 2010 EUROPA LEAGUE FINAL WITH **FULHAM**, AND RELEGATION AND PROMOTION WITH **QPR** BEFORE ENDING HIS PLAYING DAYS BACK AT **BRIGHTON**.

5 STRIKER WHO WON THE 1964 FA CUP AND 1965 EUROPEAN CUP WINNERS' CUP WITH **THE HAMMERS**, THEN MOVED ON TO **FULHAM** AND **MILLWALL** BEFORE REJOINING **WEST HAM** IN 1970.

6 DEFENDER WHO STARTED OUT AT **DONCASTER ROVERS**, AND SPENT SEVEN YEARS AT **QPR** AND FIVE AT **FULHAM**, BEFORE JOINING **WEST HAM** IN 2003. HE MOVED ON TO **PLYMOUTH ARGYLE** TWO YEARS LATER AND ENDED HIS PLAYING CAREER AT **OXFORD UNITED**.

7 DEFENDER WHOSE SEVEN YEARS IN THE SECOND AND THIRD TIER WITH **FULHAM** WERE FOLLOWED BY A DECADE AT **WEST HAM**, DURING WHICH TIME THEY WERE TWICE RELEGATED AND PROMOTED. HE WON A PREMIER LEAGUE TITLE IN HIS ONE SEASON WITH **BLACKBURN ROVERS** THEN JOINED RELEGATED **CRYSTAL PALACE**.

8 AFTER GAINING PROMOTION TO THE PREMIER LEAGUE WITH **FULHAM** IN 2018, THE FORMER **SPURS, BRENTFORD, MILLWALL, MIDDLESBROUGH** AND **BRISTOL CITY** RIGHT-BACK SIGNED TO **WEST HAM UNITED** ON A FREE TRANSFER.

HIS NAME WAS ZOLA ...

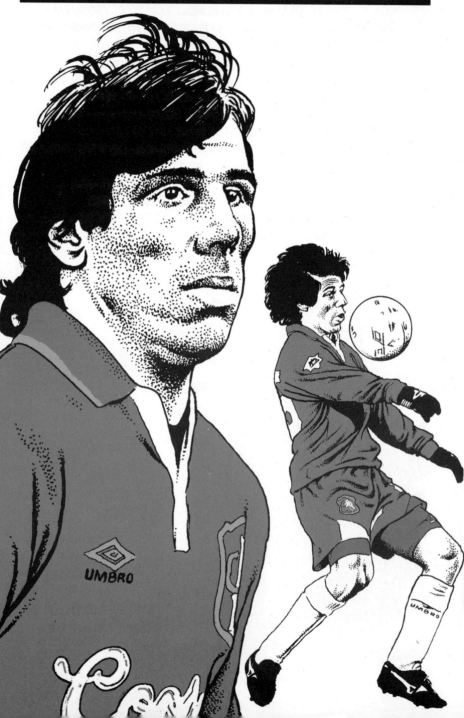

FOLLOWING A GLITTERING PLAYING CAREER THAT SAW HIM WIN A SERIE A TITLE WITH **NAPOLI**, THE UEFA CUP WITH **PARMA** AND MULTIPLE HONOURS WITH **CHELSEA** -- INCLUDING THE UEFA CUP WINNERS' CUP, TWO FA CUPS AND THE LEAGUE CUP -- **ITALY** FORWARD **GIANFRANCO ZOLA** EMBARKED ON A MANAGEMENT CAREER THAT INCLUDED SPELLS AS BOSS OF **WEST HAM**, **WATFORD** AND **BIRMINGHAM CITY**, AS WELL AS TEAMS IN ITALY AND QATAR. APPOINTED **WEST HAM** MANAGER IN 2008, HE QUICKLY FASHIONED A TEAM THAT EMBRACED SKILL AND FLAIR AND INTEGRATED A NUMBER OF YOUNGER PLAYERS. THE WHEELS CAME OFF IN HIS SECOND SEASON AND HE WAS SACKED IN 2010.

FROM WHICH CLUBS WERE THE FOLLOWING RECRUITED DURING **ZOLA'S** TENURE?

1 **SAVIO NSEREKO**

2 **ALESSANDRO DIAMANTI**

3 **RADOSLAV KOVAC**

4 **HÉRITA ILUNGA**

5 **MANUEL DA COSTA**

6 **BENNI MCCARTHY**

7 **FABIO DAPRELÀ**

8 **LUIS JIMÉNEZ**

9 **GUILLERMO FRANCO**

10 **ILAN**

11 **MIDO**

12 **DANNY UCHECHI**

CZECH HAMMERS

HAVING ARRIVED AT **WEST HAM** IN EARLY 2020, **TOMÁŠ SOUČEK** FINISHED THE 2020-21 SEASON AS JOINT TOP SCORER ON TEN GOALS WITH **MICHAIL ANTONIO** AND EARNED HIMSELF THE **HAMMER OF THE YEAR** AWARD IN THE PROCESS.

IDENTIFY THESE OTHER CZECH **HAMMERS:**

1 CENTRE-BACK WHO WON HONOURS WITH **SPARTA PRAGUE** AND **FIORENTINA** BEFORE JOINING **WEST HAM** IN 2001, HE RECEIVED TWO YELLOW CARDS ON HIS DEBUT, SETTING HIS STALL OUT FOR THE DISCIPLINARY PROBLEMS THAT MARKED HIS TIME WITH **THE HAMMERS.** HE RECEIVED 20 RED CARDS IN HIS CAREER!

2 GOALKEEPER WHO MADE 374 APPEARANCES IN HIS EIGHT YEARS WITH **WEST HAM** BEFORE SIGNING FOR **QPR** IN 1998.

3 **CZECH REPUBLIC** MIDFIELDER WHO JOINED **WEST HAM** ON LOAN FROM **SPARTAK MOSCOW** IN 2021.

4 **CZECH REPUBLIC** DEFENDER WHO, DURING HIS **SPARTAK MOSCOW** DAYS, ONCE EARNED A YELLOW CARD FOR TACKLING A PITCH INVADER. HE JOINED **THE HAMMERS** IN EARLY 2009, AND MOVED ON TO SWISS SUPER LEAGUE CHAMPIONS **BASEL** IN 2011.

5 **CZECH REPUBLIC** GOALKEEPER WHO SPENT THE MAJORITY OF HIS CAREER IN ENGLISH FOOTBALL, MAINLY WITH **NEWCASTLE UNITED** BUT ALSO WITH **SHEFFIELD WEDNESDAY**, **PORTSMOUTH** AND **WEST HAM**. HE ENDED HIS CAREER WITH A SECOND SPELL AT **NEWCASTLE** IN THE 2006-07 SEASON.

6 RIGHT-BACK WHO WON LEAGUE AND CUP HONOURS WITH **SLAVIA PRAGUE** BEFORE JOINING **WEST HAM** IN 2020 IN A £5.4 MILLION DEAL.

ROBBIE KEANE: GOAL MACHINE

IN HIS 21-YEAR CAREER **ROBBIE KEANE** PLAYED AT THE HIGHEST LEVEL IN ENGLAND, SCOTLAND, THE UNITED STATES AND ITALY, HITTING A CAREER TOTAL OF 325 GOALS IN 737 GAMES. AT INTERNATIONAL LEVEL, HE BECAME THE MOST-CAPPED PLAYER AND LEADING GOALSCORER IN REPUBLIC OF IRELAND HISTORY.

AT WHICH CLUBS DID HE PLAY UNDER THESE MANAGERS:

1 *ALEX MCLEISH*

2 *GORDON STRACHAN*

3 *BRUCE ARENA*

4 *DAVID O'LEARY*

5 *HARRY REDKNAPP*

6 *MARCELLO LIPPI*

7 *TONY MOWBRAY*

8 *TERRY VENABLES*

9 *MARK MCGHEE*

10 *RAFA BENITEZ*

BIG SAM'S GAMBLE

SAM ALLARDYCE HAD BEEN TRACKING THE PROGRESS OF *VITESSE ARNHEM* STRIKER *WILFRIED BONY* WITH THE INTENTION OF BRINGING HIM TO *WEST HAM*, WHEN THE OPPORTUNITY TO SIGN *ANDY CARROLL* FROM *LIVERPOOL* AROSE. *CARROLL'S* SEVEN SEASONS WITH *THE HAMMERS* WERE PLAGUED BY INJURY WOES. *BONY* SIGNED FOR *SWANSEA CITY*, WHERE HIS PROLIFIC FORM -- 34 GOALS IN 70 GAMES -- CAUGHT THE EYE OF *MANCHESTER CITY*. THE SUBSEQUENT MOVE WAS HUGELY DISAPPOINTING FOR ALL PARTIES, THE GOALS DRIED UP AND THE *IVORY COAST* STRIKER WAS SHIPPED OUT ON LOAN TO *STOKE CITY* BEFORE MAKING A RETURN TO *SWANSEA*, WHERE THE GOALS CONTINUED TO ELUDE HIM.

FROM WHICH CLUBS DID *SAM ALLARDYCE* SIGN THE FOLLOWING PLAYERS TO *WEST HAM?*

1 ENNER VALENCIA

2 MATT JARVIS

3 CHEIKHOU KOUYATÉ

4 STEWART DOWNING

5 AARON CRESSWELL

6 JAMES COLLINS

7 SAM BALDOCK

8 MATTHEW TAYLOR

9 NICKY MAYNARD

10 STEPHEN HENDERSON

11 RICARDO VAZ TÊ

12 EMANUEL POGATETZ

13 *JOHN CAREW*

14 *JOEY O'BRIEN*

15 *ABDOULAYE FAYE*

16 *GEORGE MCCARTNEY*

17 *MANUEL ALMUNIA*

18 *YOSSI BENAYOUN*

19 *JOE COLE*

20 *ALEX SONG*

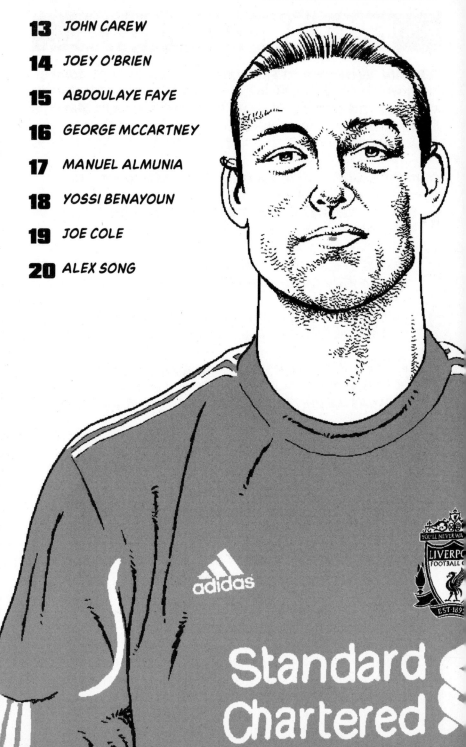

ENGLAND EXPECTS

JERMAIN DEFOE MADE HIS *ENGLAND* DEBUT IN MARCH 2004, COMING ON AS AN EARLY SUBSTITUTE FOR THE INJURED *DARIUS VASSELL* IN A 1-0 LOSS TO *SWEDEN.* HE MADE HIS FIRST START FOR *THE THREE LIONS* LATER THAT YEAR, SCORING IN A 2-1 FIFA WORLD CUP QUALIFYING WIN AGAINST *POLAND.*

IDENTIFY THESE OTHER *ENGLAND* DEBUTS BY *WEST HAM* PLAYERS:

1 MAY 20, 1962: *WEST HAM* DEFENDER AGED 21, WITHIN A YEAR HE WAS CAPTAIN OF HIS COUNTRY.

2 APRIL 3, 1974: 25-YEAR-OLD *WEST HAM* MIDFIELDER, WINNING THE FIRST OF HIS 47 CAPS -- *ALF RAMSEY'S* LAST GAME IN CHARGE.

3 MAY 8, 1976: 26-YEAR-OLD CENTRE-FORWARD WHO WOULD WIN ALL 15 OF HIS CAPS WHILE PLAYING FOR *MANCHESTER UNITED.*

4 FEBRUARY 17, 1993: *QPR* STRIKER WHO SCORED ON HIS DEBUT, HE WOULD EARN SIX MORE CAPS WHILE WITH *QPR*, SIX WITH *NEWCASTLE UNITED* AND FOUR WITH *TOTTENHAM HOTSPUR.*

5 NOVEMBER 15, 1997: 19-YEAR-OLD *WEST HAM* CENTRE-BACK WINNING THE FIRST OF 81 CAPS.

6 NOVEMBER 10, 2001: 28-YEAR-OLD *WEST HAM* MIDFIELDER WHO WOULD WIN 10 MORE CAPS WHILE WITH *THE HAMMERS* AND HIS FINAL CAP WHILE PLAYING FOR *MANCHESTER CITY.*

7 FEBRUARY 12, 2003: *CHARLTON ATHLETIC* RIGHT-BACK, HE WON ONE MORE CAP, TWO YEARS LATER, WHILE WITH *WEST HAM.*

8 MAY 31, 2005: *NORWICH CITY* GOALKEEPER, HE WOULD WIN THE LAST OF HIS 12 CAPS WHILE WITH *WEST HAM.*

9 FEBRUARY 11, 2009: *WEST HAM* STRIKER MADE THE FIRST OF HIS SEVEN APPEARANCES FOR *ENGLAND*, ALL FROM THE SUBSTITUTES' BENCH, WHICH IS, AS OF 2021, A NATIONAL RECORD.

10 NOVEMBER 17, 2010: STRIKER WHO MADE HIS DEBUT WHILE A *NEWCASTLE UNITED* PLAYER, EARNED SEVEN CAPS WHILE WITH *LIVERPOOL*, AND HIS FINAL CAP WHILE AT *WEST HAM*.

11 OCTOBER 8, 2016: *MANCHESTER UNITED* MIDFIELDER, HE WOULD LATER EARN FIVE OF HIS CAPS WHILE ON LOAN AT *WEST HAM*.

12 NOVEMBER 15, 2016: *WEST HAM* LEFT-BACK, FORMERLY WITH *TRANMERE ROVERS* AND *IPSWICH TOWN*.

13 MARCH 22, 2019: *WEST HAM* MIDFIELDER WHO PLAYED THREE SENIOR GAMES FOR *REPUBLIC OF IRELAND* BEFORE SWITCHING HIS ALLEGIANCE TO *ENGLAND*.

HOOPS! ... I DID IT AGAIN

FOLLOWING A STELLAR PLAYING CAREER THAT HAD SEEN HIM WIN AN FA CUP WITH **ARSENAL** AND TWO SERIE A TITLES WITH **JUVENTUS** -- AS WELL AS PLAY FOR **SAMPDORIA, INTERNAZIONALE** AND **ASCOLI** -- REPUBLIC OF IRELAND MIDFIELDER **LIAM BRADY** ENDED HIS PLAYING DAYS AT **WEST HAM.** UNFORTUNATELY, HE COULDN'T HELP **THE IRONS** ESCAPE RELEGATION AND HE HUNG UP HIS PLAYING BOOTS IN 1990. HE LAUNCHED HIS MANAGEMENT CAREER AT **CELTIC** IN 1991.

IDENTIFY THESE OTHER **WEST HAM** CONNECTIONS TO **CELTIC**:

1 WHICH STRIKER, A THREE-TIME WELSH FOOTBALLER OF THE YEAR, LAUNCHED HIS CAREER AT **LUTON TOWN**, BECAME BRITAIN'S MOST EXPENSIVE TEENAGER WHEN HE SIGNED FOR **ARSENAL**, AND **WEST HAM'S** RECORD SIGNING WHEN HE JOINED IN 1997? AFTER PLAYING FOR **WIMBLEDON** AND **COVENTRY CITY**, HE WON MULTIPLE HONOURS WITH **CELTIC**, WHERE HE WAS NAMED BOTH PFA SCOTLAND PLAYERS' PLAYER OF THE YEAR AND SFWA FOOTBALLER OF THE YEAR IN 2005.

2 WHICH **WEST HAM** MANAGER WON MULTIPLE HONOURS WITH **CELTIC** AND **MANCHESTER UNITED** BEFORE ENDING HIS PLAYING DAYS AT **SWINDON TOWN?**

3 WHICH **SCOTLAND** STRIKER JOINED **WEST HAM** FROM **ST MIRREN** IN 1985, SIGNED FOR **CELTIC** IN 1987, WON A LEAGUE AND CUP DOUBLE WITH **"THE BHOYS"** BEFORE RETURNING TO **WEST HAM** IN 1989 ... AND THEN REJOINED **CELTIC** IN 1992?

4 WHICH **WEST HAM** MANAGER BEGAN HIS PLAYING CAREER AT **CELTIC**, ENDING IT 19 YEARS LATER WITH **PRESTON NORTH END?**

5 WHICH **ISRAEL** INTERNATIONAL MIDFIELDER LEFT **WEST HAM** FOR **CELTIC** IN 1999?

THE CHAMPIONS

FLORIN RĂDUCIOIU MADE JUST A HANDFUL OF APPEARANCES DURING HIS SEASON WITH **AC MILAN** IN 1993-94 -- BUT THEY WERE ENOUGH TO EARN HIM SERIE A AND UEFA CHAMPIONS LEAGUE WINNER MEDALS.

WITH WHICH TEAMS DID THESE **HAMMERS** WIN THE UEFA CHAMPIONS LEAGUE?

1   TEDDY SHERINGHAM

2   NEIL MELLOR

3   DAVOR ŠUKER

4   KURT ZOUMA

5   CARLOS TEVEZ

6   BENNI MCCARTHY

7   ÁLVARO ARBELOA

FWA FOOTBALLER OF THE YEAR

SINCE 1948, THE MEMBERS OF THE FOOTBALL WRITERS' ASSOCIATION -- APPROXIMATELY 400 FOOTBALL JOURNALISTS -- HAVE VOTED ON THE PLAYER OF THE YEAR. THE FIRST **WEST HAM** PLAYER TO WIN THE FWA FOOTBALLER OF THE YEAR AWARD WAS **BOBBY MOORE** IN 1964.

IDENTIFY THESE OTHER WINNERS WITH **WEST HAM** LINKS:

1 1987: STRIKER WHO WON THE AWARD WHILE WITH **TOTTENHAM HOTSPUR**, HE SIGNED FOR **THE HAMMERS** IN 1992.

2 1997: WON THE AWARD WHILE PLAYING FOR **CHELSEA**, HE WAS APPOINTED **WEST HAM** MANAGER ELEVEN YEARS LATER.

3 2001: FORWARD WHO WON THE AWARD THE YEAR HE REJOINED **TOTTENHAM HOTSPUR** FROM **MANCHESTER UNITED** AND THREE YEARS BEFORE HE SIGNED FOR **WEST HAM**.

4 2005: FORMER **HAMMER** WHO WON WHILE WITH **CHELSEA**.

5 2011: **WEST HAM** AND **ENGLAND** MIDFIELDER.

HAMMER HART

THE ARRIVAL OF **PEP GUARDIOLA** WAS A COUP FOR **MANCHESTER CITY** BUT A SETBACK FOR **JOE HART**. THE **ENGLAND** GOALKEEPER HAD WON TWO PREMIER LEAGUE TITLES AND THREE DOMESTIC CUPS WITH **CITY**, WHILE WINNING FOUR PREMIER LEAGUE GOLDEN GLOVES. THE SPANIARD'S ARRIVAL SAW **HART** SHIPPED OUT ON LOAN TO **TORINO** AND **WEST HAM**, FOLLOWED BY MOVES TO **BURNLEY** AND **SPURS**. NONE OF THE MOVES COULD BE DEEMED A SUCCESS. HE JOINED **CELTIC** IN 2020.

HART WAS A **SLAVEN BILIĆ** SIGNING FOR **WEST HAM**, AS WERE THE FOLLOWING. FROM WHICH CLUBS WERE THEY SIGNED?

1 MICHAIL ANTONIO

2 ANDRÉ AYEW

3 MARKO ARNAUTOVIĆ

4 JAVIER HERNÁNDEZ

5 DIMITRI PAYET

6 MANUEL LANZINI

7 ROBERT SNODGRASS

8 ANGELO OGBONNA

9 JOSÉ FONTE

10 ARTHUR MASUAKU

11 EDIMILSON FERNANDES

12 PEDRO OBIANG

13 SAM BYRAM

14 JONATHAN CALLERI

15 NIKICA JELAVIĆ

16 GÖKHAN TÖRE

17 SEAD HAKŠABANOVIĆ

18 STEPHEN HENDRIE

19 EMMANUEL EMENIKE

20 DARREN RANDOLPH

21 HÅVARD NORDTVEIT

22 ÁLVARO ARBELOA

23 SOFIANE FEGHOULI

24 PABLO ZABALETA

HAMMERS ON THE BOX

AFTER HANGING UP HIS PLAYING BOOTS, *FRANK LAMPARD* SERVED AS A TEAM CAPTAIN ON THE ITV SPORT PANEL SHOW *"PLAY TO THE WHISTLE"* FROM 2015 UNTIL 2017.

IDENTIFY THESE *HAMMERS* FROM THEIR TV CREDITS:

1 WHICH FORMER *WEST HAM* FULL-BACK WAS CROWNED WINNER OF THE FIRST SERIES OF *"CELEBRITY SAS: WHO DARES WINS"*?

2 WHICH *WEST HAM* AND *ENGLAND* GOALKEEPER PARTNERED *NADIYA BYCHKOVA* ON *"STRICTLY COME DANCING 2019"*?

3 WHICH *WEST HAM* AND *ENGLAND* STAR'S TV CREDITS INCLUDE CAPTAINING A TEAM ON *"THEY THINK IT'S ALL OVER"*, AND HOSTING *"FRIENDS LIKE THESE"* AND *"MONEYBALL"*?

4 WHICH *HAMMER* WAS CROWNED KING OF THE JUNGLE ON *"I'M A CELEBRITY... GET ME OUT OF HERE!"* IN 2018?

5 WHICH *WEST HAM* FORWARD WAS A TEAM CAPTAIN ON *"SPORTING TRIANGLES"* OPPOSITE *ANDY GRAY* AND *EMLYN HUGHES*?

6 WHICH *WEST HAM* HARDMAN REACHED THE FINAL THREE ON BBC'S *"CELEBRITY MASTERCHEF"* IN 2019?

FRENCH IMPORTS

ISSA DIOP -- A CLUB RECORD £22 MILLION SIGNING FROM *TOULOUSE* IN 2018 -- BECAME THE FIRST CONCUSSION SUBSTITUTE IN ENGLISH FOOTBALL WHEN, DURING AN FA CUP GAME AGAINST *MANCHESTER UNITED* IN 2021, HE WAS REPLACED BY *RYAN FREDERICKS* FOLLOWING A HEAD INJURY.

FROM WHICH FRENCH CLUBS WERE THESE *HAMMERS* SIGNED?

1 *ALPHONSE AREOLA* -- 2021

2 *DIMITRI PAYET* -- 2015

3 *FRÉDÉRIC KANOUTÉ* -- 2000

4 *DIAFRA SAKHO* -- 2014

5 *ILAN* -- 2010

6 *BERNARD LAMA* -- 1997

7 *JULIEN FAUBERT* -- 2007

8 *HÉRITA ILUNGA* -- 2021

9 *ÉDOUARD CISSÉ* -- 2002

10 *FRÉDÉRIC PIQUIONNE* -- 2010

THE TENACIOUS ONE

CRAIG BELLAMY WON HONOURS WITH *LIVERPOOL, CELTIC* AND *CARDIFF CITY* IN A CAREER THAT SAW HIM SCORE 170 GOALS IN 549 GAMES. AT WHICH CLUB DID HE PLAY UNDER MANAGER:

1   *SIR KENNY DALGLISH*

2   *SIR BOBBY ROBSON*

3   *MARTIN O'NEILL*

4   *GIANFRANCO ZOLA*

5   *DAVE JONES*

6   *ROBERTO MANCINI*

7   *BRUCE RIOCH*

8   *GORDON STRACHAN*

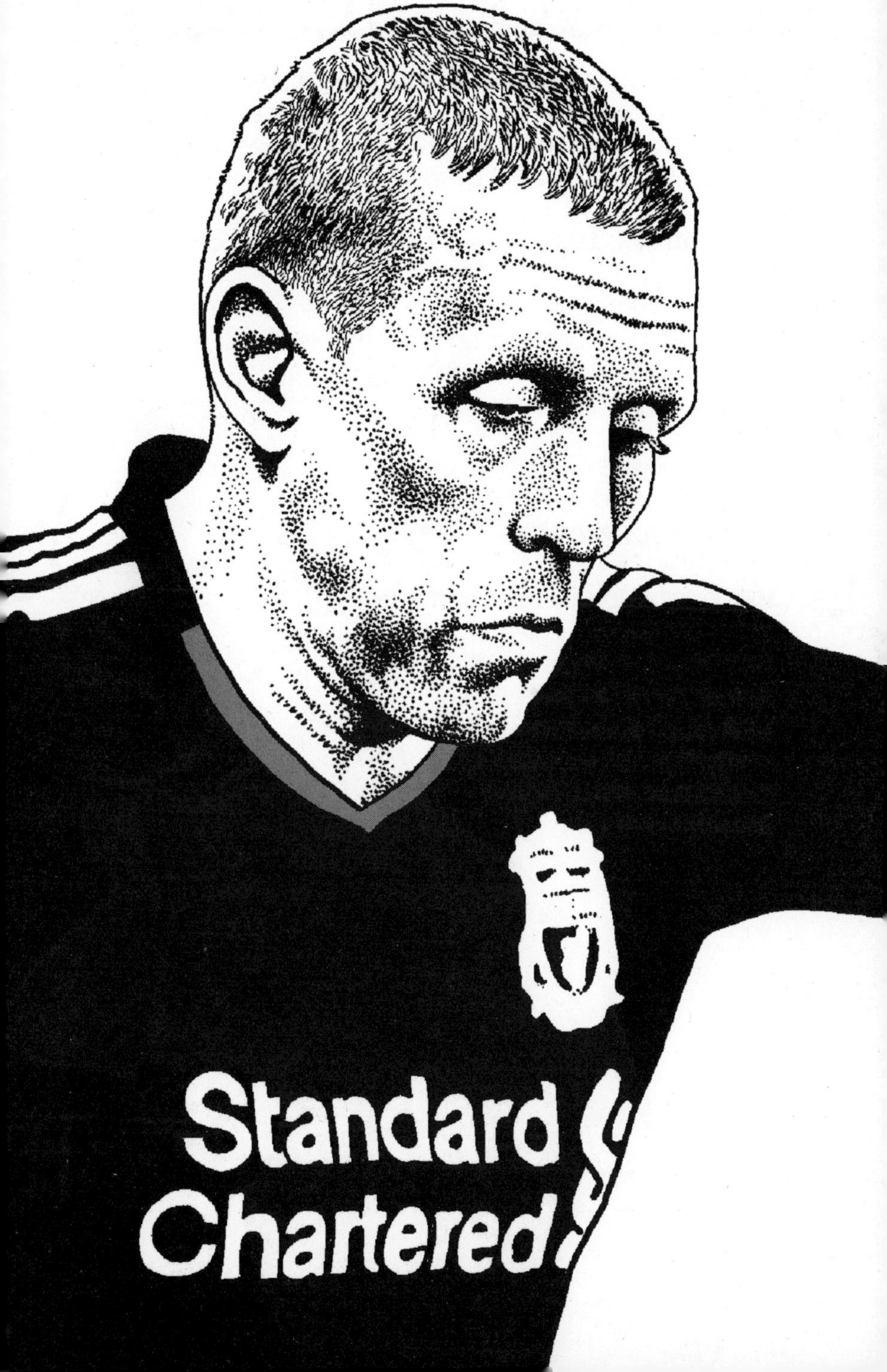
Standard
Chartered

MARCHING ON TOGETHER

THE £18 MILLION THAT *LEEDS UNITED* PAID TO SIGN *WEST HAM'S RIO FERDINAND* IN 2000 WAS NOT ONLY A BRITISH TRANSFER RECORD, IT MADE THE CENTRE-BACK, WHO HAD JUST TURNED 22 YEARS OLD, THE WORLD'S MOST EXPENSIVE DEFENDER TO THAT POINT.

NAME THESE OTHER *HAMMERS* WHO PLAYED FOR *LEEDS UNITED*:

1 SCORER OF THE FIRST-EVER GOAL IN THE PREMIER LEAGUE IN 1992, IN THE FIRST OF THREE SPELLS WITH *SHEFFIELD UNITED*, HE HAD TWO SPELLS AT *LEEDS* AND PLAYED FOR *WEST HAM* IN THE 2003-04 SEASON.

2 RIGHT-BACK WHO SPENT FOUR SEASONS AT *LEEDS*, JOINED *WEST HAM* IN 2016 AND THEN *NORWICH CITY* IN 2019.

3 MIDFIELDER WHO SPENT THE MAJORITY OF HIS CAREER AT *LEEDS UNITED*, HAD TWO SPELLS AT *WEST HAM* EITHER SIDE OF THREE SEASONS WITH *NEWCASTLE UNITED*, AND HAS PLAYED FOR AND MANAGED BOTH *CHARLTON ATHLETIC* AND *BIRMINGHAM CITY*.

4 CENTRE-BACK WHO CAME THROUGH THE RANKS AT **LEEDS**, HAD A BRIEF LOAN SPELL AT **WEST HAM** IN 2003, AND WENT ON TO PLAY FOR CLUBS IN ENGLAND, SCOTLAND AND INDIA, INCLUDING **SHEFFIELD UNITED**, **SUNDERLAND** AND **BLACKBURN ROVERS**.

5 **ENGLAND** GOALKEEPER WHO DROPPED A CLANGER AT THE 2010 WORLD CUP, WON HONOURS WITH **NORWICH CITY**, **WEST HAM** AND **QPR** AND SPENT A LITTLE OVER A SEASON AT **LEEDS**.

6 **NORTHERN IRELAND** DEFENDER WHO YO-YOED BETWEEN **SUNDERLAND** AND **WEST HAM**, WINNING PROMOTIONS WITH BOTH. HE ALSO SPENT TIME ON LOAN AT **LEEDS**.

7 **SCOTLAND** WINGER WHO WON PROMOTIONS WITH **LEEDS** AND **HULL CITY**, EITHER SIDE OF SPELLS WITH **NORWICH CITY**, **WEST HAM** AND **ASTON VILLA**, BEFORE JOINING **WEST BROM** IN 2021.

8 **WEST HAM** ACADEMY GRADUATE WINGER WHO HAD LOAN SPELLS AT A NUMBER OF CLUBS, INCLUDING **LEEDS** AND **CHARLTON ATHLETIC**, FOLLOWING HIS 2008 MOVE TO **QPR**.

9 STRIKER WHO PLAYED FOR A DOZEN ENGLISH CLUBS, INCLUDING **ARSENAL** AND **WEST HAM**, HE WON HONOURS WITH **NOTTINGHAM FOREST** AND **LEEDS** AND LATER BECAME A SUCCESSFUL RESTAURANT OWNER.

10 SCORER OF 68 GOALS IN 146 GAMES FOR THE **REPUBLIC OF IRELAND**.

THE CENTURIONS

WINNER OF THREE UKRAINIAN PREMIER LEAGUE TITLES AND NUMEROUS CUPS WITH **DYNAMO KYIV**, **ANDRIY YARMOLENKO** SIGNED FOR **WEST HAM** IN 2018, AFTER WHICH HE WAS PLAGUED BY SERIOUS INJURIES AND STRUGGLED TO FIND FORM. AT INTERNATIONAL LEVEL, HE MADE HIS 100TH APPEARANCE FOR **UKRAINE** IN SEPTEMBER, 2021.

IDENTIFY THE FOLLOWING **HAMMERS** WHO GAINED A CENTURY OF INTERNATIONAL CAPS:

1 *147* FOR **ARGENTINA** (2003-2018)

2 *146* FOR **REPUBLIC OF IRELAND** (1998-2016)

3 *137* FOR **CAMEROON** (1993-2010)

4 *125* FOR **ENGLAND** (1970-1990)

5 *113* FOR **ROMANIA** (2002-2016)

6 *109* FOR **SWEDEN** (1993-2008)

7 *109* FOR **MEXICO** (2009-2019)

8 *108* FOR **ENGLAND** (1962-1973)

9 *106* FOR **ENGLAND** (1999-2014)

10 *101* FOR **ISRAEL** (1998-2017)

MONIKERS

AT THE OUTSET OF HIS CAREER, *TREVOR BROOKING* WAS NICKNAMED *"CYRIL"* BY HIS TEAMMATES FOR THE CARPET MANUFACTURER *CYRIL LORD*, AFTER MANAGER *RON GREENWOOD* TOLD THE SLIGHT YOUNGSTER HE WAS *"ALWAYS ON THE FLOOR."* FOR A TIME, *BROOKING'S* LACK OF PACE SAW HIM REFERRED TO AS *"BOOG"*, AFTER A SLOW-FOOTED BASEBALL PLAYER CALLED *BOOG POWELL* THAT THE TEAM HAD WATCHED ON A TOUR OF THE STATES. EVENTUALLY, HE CAME TO BE KNOWN AS *"HADLEIGH"*, A NICKNAME INSPIRED BY A TV SERIES STARRING *GERALD HARPER* AS A GENTLEMANLY COUNTRY SQUIRE.

IDENTIFY THE FOLLOWING *WEST HAM* PLAYERS FROM THEIR NICKNAMES:

1   *"STRETCH"*

2   *"RAZOR"*

3   *"CHIPPY"*

4   *"TONKA"*

5   *"BUDGIE"*

6   *"MUFFIN"*

7   *"PUFFER"*

8   *"ONE SIZE"*

9   *"TICKER"*

10   *"STAG"*

11   *"THE GENERAL"*

12   *"EL APACHE"*

13   *"BONZO"*

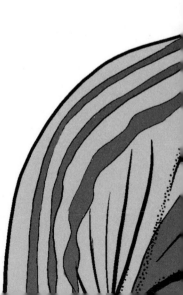

ROEDER'S RECRUITS

DAVID JAMES JOINED **WEST HAM** FROM **ASTON VILLA** IN THE SUMMER OF 2001, DAYS INTO THE TENURE OF NEW MANAGER **GLENN ROEDER**. A KNEE INJURY SUSTAINED ON INTERNATIONAL DUTY WITH **ENGLAND** KEPT THE £3.5 MILLION SIGNING ON THE SIDELINES UNTIL LATE NOVEMBER.

IDENTIFY THESE OTHER **GLENN ROEDER** ACQUISITIONS, SIGNED BETWEEN 2001 AND 2003:

1   CENTRE-BACK FROM *FIORENTINA* -- £5.5 MILLION

2   MIDFIELDER FROM *SUNDERLAND* -- £5 MILLION

3   LEFT-BACK FROM *SPARTA PRAGUE* -- £1 MILLION

4   MIDFIELDER FROM *MANCHESTER CITY* -- £300,000

5   STRIKER FROM *WIMBLEDON* -- £285,000

6   MIDFIELDER FROM *NEWCASTLE* -- SECOND SPELL AT *WEST HAM*

7   GOALKEEPER FROM *BARRY TOWN* -- FREE TRANSFER

8   MIDFIELDER FROM *ARSENAL* -- FREE TRANSFER

9   GOALKEEPER FROM *MANCHESTER UNITED* -- FREE TRANSFER

10   DEFENDER FROM *FULHAM* -- UNDISCLOSED FEE

11   STRIKER FROM *LIVERPOOL* -- LOAN TRANSFER

12   CENTRE-BACK FROM *LEEDS UNITED* -- LOAN TRANSFER

13   STRIKER FROM *TOTTENHAM HOTSPUR* -- UNDISCLOSED FEE

14   CENTRE-BACK FROM *COVENTRY CITY* -- FREE TRANSFER

15   MIDFIELDER FROM *LYON* -- FREE TRANSFER

16   LEFT-WINGER FROM *TOTTENHAM HOTSPUR* -- EXCHANGE DEAL

THE MIDDLE MEN

PAUL INCE'S FULL NAME IS **PAUL EMERSON CARLYLE INCE.**
JERMAIN DEFOE'S MIDDLE NAME IS **COLIN.** SEE IF YOU CAN IDENTIFY
THESE **WEST HAM** PLAYERS BY THEIR MIDDLE NAMES:

1 STANFORD

2 MCLEOD COOPER

3 EUCHURIA CORNELIUS

4 GAVIN

5 HAPPY

6 MAREK

7 ALIEU

8 FREDERICK CHELSEA

9 LÉOPOLD

10 ANTHONY JANCE

11 CHINEYE

12 STRUAN MCDONALD

13 SHOLA ANDRE

14 PEACE

15 TAFARI

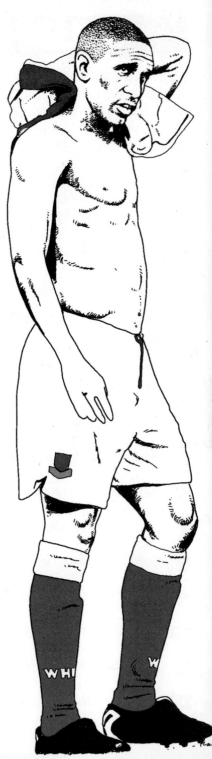

HELLO GOODBYE!

GLENN ROEDER'S TIME AS WEST HAM BOSS WAS MARKED BY THE LOSS OF SOME OF THE CLUB'S MOST PROMISING TALENT. APPOINTED IN THE SUMMER OF 2001, FOLLOWING THE DEPARTURE OF HARRY REDKNAPP, ROEDER IMMEDIATELY LOST A DISGRUNTLED FRANK LAMPARD TO CHELSEA. WITH THE TEAM STRUGGLING DURING HIS SECOND SEASON, ROEDER WAS DIAGNOSED WITH A BRAIN TUMOUR. BY THE TIME HE RETURNED TO WORK, WEST HAM WERE PRETTY MUCH DOOMED TO RELEGATION. THAT SUMMER, HE LOST JOE COLE AND GLEN JOHNSON TO CHELSEA, TREVOR SINCLAIR TO MANCHESTER CITY AND FRÉDÉRIC KANOUTÉ TO SPURS. ROEDER WAS SACKED THREE GAMES INTO THE NEW SEASON IN THE SECOND TIER.

WHICH MANAGERS OVERSAW THE DEPARTURE OF THE FOLLOWING?

1 AUGUST, 2011: SCOTT PARKER TO TOTTENHAM HOTSPUR

2 JANUARY, 2018: ANDRÉ AYEW TO SWANSEA CITY

3 SEPTEMBER, 1989: PAUL INCE TO MANCHESTER UNITED

4 AUGUST, 2004: MICHAEL CARRICK TO TOTTENHAM HOTSPUR

5 MARCH, 1974: BOBBY MOORE TO FULHAM

6 SEPTEMBER, 2009: JAMES COLLINS TO ASTON VILLA

7 JULY, 2015: STEWART DOWNING TO MIDDLESBROUGH

8 JULY, 2007: NIGEL REO-COKER TO ASTON VILLA

9 AUGUST, 2018: CHEIKHOU KOUYATÉ TO CRYSTAL PALACE

10 SEPTEMBER, 1993: JULIAN DICKS TO LIVERPOOL

11 JANUARY, 1999: JOHN HARTSON TO WIMBLEDON

12 JULY, 1987: FRANK MCAVENNIE TO CELTIC

PARDEW'S PURCHASES

ALAN *PARDEW* WAS THE MANAGER WHEN 22-YEAR-OLDS *CARLOS TEVEZ* AND *JAVIER MASCHERANO* JOINED *WEST HAM* FROM *CORINTHIANS* IN 2006. THE PAIR STRUGGLED FOR GAME TIME UNDER *PARDEW*, WITH THE LIKES OF *HAYDEN MULLINS* AND *MARLON HAREWOOD* AHEAD IN THE PECKING ORDER. WITH *THE HAMMERS* IN FREEFALL, *PARDEW* WAS SOON OUT OF A JOB. *MASCHERANO* JUMPED AT THE CHANCE TO HIGHTAIL IT TO *LIVERPOOL* WHILE *TEVEZ*, RESTORED TO THE SIDE, SCORED THE GOALS THAT KEPT *THE HAMMERS* IN THE TOP FLIGHT BEFORE JOINING *MANCHESTER UNITED*. THE TWO *ARGENTINA* STARS WENT ON TO AMASS A PLETHORA OF HONOURS, BOTH WINNING THE UEFA CHAMPIONS LEAGUE, *TEVEZ* WINNING LEAGUE TITLES WITH *UNITED*, *MANCHESTER CITY* AND *JUVENTUS*, *MASCHERANO* WINNING LA LIGA FIVE TIMES WITH *BARCELONA*.

FROM WHICH CLUBS WERE THE FOLLOWING SIGNED UNDER *PARDEW?*

1 *DEAN ASHTON*

2 *YOSSI BENAYOUN*

3 *CARLTON COLE*

4 *ROB GREEN*

5 *PAUL KONCHESKY*

6 *DANNY GABBIDON*

7 *JAMES COLLINS*

8 *GEORGE MCCARTNEY*

9 *TYRONE MEARS*

10 *JOHN PAINTSIL*

11 *NIGEL REO-COKER*

A CHANGE OF HEART

ALTHOUGH BORN IN LONDON, *DECLAN RICE* -- THE GRANDSON OF CORK NATIVES -- OPTED TO PLAY FOR THE *REPUBLIC OF IRELAND*, REPRESENTING THE COUNTRY AT A NUMBER OF YOUTH LEVELS. IN 2018, HE PLAYED IN THREE SENIOR FRIENDLY GAMES FOR THE *REPUBLIC*, BEFORE A CHANGE OF HEART SAW HIM SWITCH ALLEGIANCE TO *ENGLAND*. HE MADE HIS DEBUT FOR THE *THREE LIONS* IN 2019.

IDENTIFY THE COUNTRY OTHER THAN THEIR OWN THAT THESE OTHER *HAMMERS* CHOSE TO PLAY FOR:

1 *JULIEN FAUBERT* (BORN IN FRANCE)

2 *MICHAIL ANTONIO* (BORN IN ENGLAND)

3 *RAY HOUGHTON* (BORN IN SCOTLAND)

4 *DEMBA BA* (BORN IN FRANCE)

5 *JACK COLLISON* (BORN IN ENGLAND)

6 *FRÉDÉRIC KANOUTÉ* (BORN IN FRANCE)

7 *RAVEL MORRISON* (BORN IN ENGLAND)

8 *ANDRÉ AYEW* (BORN IN FRANCE)

9 *IAIN DOWIE* (BORN IN ENGLAND)

10 *SHAKA HISLOP* (BORN IN ENGLAND)

11 *SOFIANE FEGHOULI* (BORN IN FRANCE)

12 *CHRIS HUGHTON* (BORN IN ENGLAND)

13 *MAROUANE CHAMAKH* (BORN IN FRANCE)

14 *STEVE LOMAS* (BORN IN WEST GERMANY)

POACHERS TURNED GAMEKEEPERS

AS A PLAYER, *IGOR STIMAC* WAS CAPPED 53 TIMES BY *CROATIA* AND HAD THREE DIFFERENT SPELLS WITH *HAJDUK SPLIT*. HE THEN LAUNCHED HIS MANAGEMENT CAREER WITH THE CLUB IN 2005 AND WAS APPOINTED *CROATIA* NATIONAL TEAM MANAGER IN 2012.

NAME THESE **WEST HAM** PLAYERS WHO ALSO PLAYED FOR AND
MANAGED THE SAME CLUB:

1   **CHELSEA**: PLAYED 2001-14 AND MANAGED 2019-21

2   **CRYSTAL PALACE**: PLAYED 1995 AND MANAGED 2003-06

3   **MANCHESTER CITY**: PLAYED 2001-02 AND MANAGED 2005-07

4   **BOURNEMOUTH**: PLAYED 1972-76 AND MANAGED 1983-92

5   **CHARLTON ATHLETIC**: PLAYED 1994-96 AND MANAGED 2018-21

6   **STEAUA BUCUREȘTI**: PLAYED 1986-94 AND MANAGED 2010

7   **WATFORD**: PLAYED 2005-08 AND MANAGED 2009-11

8   **CHARLTON ATHLETIC**: PLAYED 1998-2004, 2005-06, 2007-08
AND MANAGED 2011-14

9   **LEYTON ORIENT**: PLAYED 1956-57 AND MANAGED 1965

10   **HEREDIANO**: PLAYED 1993-97, 2006 AND MANAGED 2008-09

11   **CHELSEA**: PLAYED 1968-74 AND MANAGED 1993

12   **CARLISLE UNITED**: PLAYED 1993-94 AND MANAGED 1996-97

SHOW US YOUR MEDALS

HAVING WON THE 2013 COUPE DE LA LIGUE WITH **SAINT-ÉTIENNE**, FOR WHOM HE MADE HIS DEBUT AT THE AGE OF 16, **KURT ZOUMA** JOINED **CHELSEA** IN 2014. THE CLUB'S YOUNG PLAYER OF THE YEAR IN HIS DEBUT SEASON, HIS HONOURS WITH THE CLUB INCLUDE THE UEFA CHAMPIONS LEAGUE, TWO PREMIER LEAGUE TITLES, THE LEAGUE CUP AND THE UEFA SUPER CUP, ALTHOUGH SOME OF HIS TIME WITH THE CLUB WAS SPENT ON LOAN AT **STOKE CITY** AND **EVERTON**. **ZOUMA**, WHO JOINED **WEST HAM** FOR £29.8 MILLION IN 2021, MADE HIS DEBUT FOR **FRANCE** IN 2015.

NAME THE TEAM WITH WHICH THESE **WEST HAM** PLAYERS WON THE FOOTBALL LEAGUE CUP:

1 *STUART PEARCE*

2 *DAN PETRESCU*

3 *LEE BOWYER*

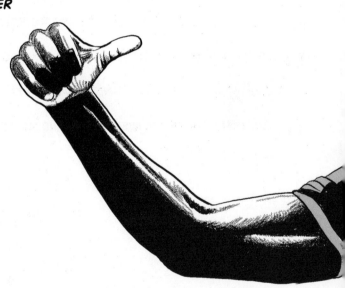

4 ROBBIE KEANE

5 RAY HOUGHTON

6 LEE CHAPMAN

7 GARY CHARLES

8 CRAIG BELLAMY

9 SAMIR NASRI

10 MARTIN PETERS

CAPE CRUSADERS!

SCORER OF **SOUTH AFRICA'S** FIRST-EVER GOAL AT A WORLD CUP, IN A 1-1 DRAW AGAINST **DENMARK** IN 1998, **BENNI MCCARTHY** WAS CAPPED 79 TIMES BY **"BAFANA BAFANA".**

A LEAGUE AND CUP WINNER WITH **AJAX**, HE WON MULTIPLE HONOURS WITH **PORTO** -- INCLUDING THE 2004 UEFA CHAMPIONS LEAGUE -- BEFORE SPENDING FOUR SEASONS AT **BLACKBURN ROVERS**. HE JOINED **WEST HAM** IN EARLY 2010 BUT HIS TIME AT **UPTON PARK** WAS BLIGHTED BY INJURY AND HE RETURNED TO HIS HOMELAND IN 2011, PLAYING FOR **ORLANDO PIRATES** BEFORE EMBARKING ON A COACHING AND MANAGEMENT CAREER.

NAME THESE **WEST HAM** PLAYERS WITH SOUTH AFRICA LINKS:

1 **ENGLAND** STRIKER WHO WON THE FA CUP WITH **THE HAMMERS** IN 1964, HE PLAYED FOR FORMER CLUB **CRYSTAL PALACE** AND HAD A SEASON AT **FULHAM** BEFORE EMIGRATING TO SOUTH AFRICA IN 1969. HE PLAYED FOR AND THEN COACHED **DURBAN CITY**, BEFORE COACHING **HELLENIC CITY, CAPE TOWN SPURS** AND **MICHAU WARRIORS**. HE DIED OF A HEART ATTACK IN CAPE TOWN IN 1999, AT THE AGE OF 60.

2 **PORTUGAL** WINGER, HE WON HONOURS WITH **ARSENAL** AND **FULHAM**, PLAYED FOR **SOUTHAMPTON**, HAD FIVE SEASONS AT **WEST HAM** AND SPENT A FEW BRIEF MONTHS WITH **ORLANDO PIRATES** BEFORE JOINING **CHESTERFIELD** IN 2012.

3 A FOOTBALLING KNIGHT WHO WON HONOURS WITH **ENGLAND** AND **WEST HAM**, HE JOINED **WEST BROMWICH ALBION** IN 1975 FROM **STOKE CITY** AFTER A LOAN SPELL WITH **CAPE TOWN CITY**.

4 FA CUP AND EUROPEAN CUP WINNERS' CUP WINNER WITH **WEST HAM** BEFORE HIS CAREER TOOK HIM TO **SHEFFIELD WEDNESDAY, NORWICH CITY, CHELSEA, TAMPA BAY ROWDIES** AND **CAPE TOWN CITY**.

5 **NIGERIA** INTERNATIONAL STRIKER WHO LAUNCHED HIS PROFESSIONAL CAREER IN SOUTH AFRICA WITH **MPUMALANGA BLACK ACES** AND **CAPE TOWN**, BEFORE PLYING HIS TRADE IN TURKEY, RUSSIA, ABU DHABI, ENGLAND, GREECE, SPAIN AND BELGIUM. HIS 2016 LOAN SPELL WITH **WEST HAM** YIELDED JUST TWO GOALS, IN A 5-1 FA CUP WIN AGAINST **BLACKBURN ROVERS**.

6 **WEST HAM** LEGEND WHOSE LATER CAREER SAW HIM PLAY WITH **FULHAM**, IN THE UNITED STATES, DENMARK AND AUSTRALIA, AND BRIEFLY WITH SOUTH AFRICA'S **HELLENIC**.

7 GOALKEEPER WHOSE CLUBS INCLUDED **COVENTRY CITY, MANCHESTER CITY, CRYSTAL PALACE, WEST HAM, BRENTFORD** AND **WATFORD**, WHO PLAYED IN SOUTH AFRICA IN THE '90S WITH **WITS UNIVERSITY** AND **SUPERSPORT UNITED**.

TEEN TITANS

AT 15, **MARK NOBLE** BECAME THE YOUNGEST PLAYER TO APPEAR FOR THE **WEST HAM** RESERVE TEAM. HE MADE THE FIRST OF HIS MORE THAN 500 OF SENIOR APPEARANCES IN 2004 AT THE AGE OF 17.

IDENTIFY THESE OTHER PLAYERS WHO WERE TEENAGERS WHEN THEY MADE THEIR DEBUTS IN THE **WEST HAM** FIRST TEAM:

1 HE BECAME **WEST HAM'S** YOUNGEST DEBUTANT WHEN HE PLAYED HIS FIRST SENIOR GAME, AGED 16 YEARS AND 198 DAYS OLD, IN A EUROPA LEAGUE QUALIFIER AGAINST **FC LUSITANOS** IN 2015.

2 PRODIGY WHO SCORED SEVEN GOALS IN ONE GAME FOR **ENGLAND SCHOOLBOYS**, HE MADE HIS FIRST TEAM DEBUT AT THE AGE OF 17 YEARS AND 63 DAYS AGAINST **MANCHESTER UNITED** IN EARLY 1999, LAUNCHING A CAREER THAT BROUGHT 56 **ENGLAND** CAPS.

3 DEBUTED FOR **THE HAMMERS** IN A 3-2 WIN OVER **SUNDERLAND** IN 2003 AT THE AGE OF 16 YEARS AND 283 DAYS, A MIDFIELDER WHO WENT ON TO MAKE MORE THAN 300 APPEARANCES FOR **NOTTINGHAM FOREST**.

4 AN UNUSED SUBSTITUTE AT THE AGE OF 16, A FUTURE **WEST HAM** MANAGER WHO MADE HIS SENIOR DEBUT FOR THE TEAM IN 1974 AT THE AGE OF 17 YEARS AND 144 DAYS.

5 PROLIFIC STRIKER WHO SCORED ON HIS **WEST HAM** DEBUT IN 1983 AGED 17 YEARS AND 176 DAYS, SPENT SIX SEASONS AT **EVERTON**, RETURNED TO **WEST HAM** BEFORE WINNING THE 2000 LEAGUE CUP WITH **LEICESTER CITY**.

SAY WHAT?

THE 1970 WORLD CUP NOT ONLY PRODUCED ONE OF THE GREAT GAMES IN WORLD CUP HISTORY, IT FEATURED ONE OF THE MOST MEMORABLE BATTLES, PITTING **ENGLAND** CAPTAIN **BOBBY MOORE** AGAINST **BRAZIL** SUPERSTAR **PELÉ. BRAZIL** DEFEATED THE REIGNING CHAMPIONS 1-0 AND WENT ON TO WIN THE TOURNAMENT. **PELÉ** LATER REMARKED, WHEN ASKED ABOUT THE BEST OPPONENTS HE EVER FACED: *"THE GREATEST DEFENDER I EVER PLAYED AGAINST."*

WHO SAID THE FOLLOWING?

1 *"THE MAN WHO COMES TO TAKE CARE OF MY PIRANHAS TOLD ME THAT IF I LEFT WEST HAM HE WOULD KILL ALL MY FISH."*

2 *"THE KEEPER WAS LIKE A RABBIT IN THE HEADLINES."*

3 *"I UNDERSTAND NOTHING WHEN RIO (FERDINAND) AND FRANK (LAMPARD) ARE TALKING. THEY SPEAK COCKNIK."*

4 *"I'VE BEEN PLAYING IN A GOLF DAY FOR A BOY SERIOUSLY INJURED IN A CAR ACCIDENT. I HAD TO DRIVE LIKE A LUNATIC TO GET HERE."*

5 *"GEOFF HURST HAD A HAMMER IN HIS LEFT BOOT AND GOOD LEFT FEET ARE LIKE BRICKS OF GOLD."*

6 *"MARTIN PETERS IS 10 YEARS AHEAD OF HIS TIME IN THE GAME."*

7 *"THIS IS FOOTBALL FROM THE 19TH CENTURY. IT'S VERY DIFFICULT TO PLAY A FOOTBALL MATCH WHEN ONLY ONE TEAM WANTS TO PLAY. A FOOTBALL MATCH IS ABOUT TWO TEAMS PLAYING. I TOLD BIG SAM, THEY NEED POINTS. TO COME HERE THE WAY THEY DID, IS THAT ACCEPTABLE? MAYBE IT IS, THEY NEED POINTS. THE ONLY THING I COULD BRING MORE WAS BLACK & DECKER - A BLACK & DECKER TO DESTROY THE WEST HAM WALL."*

8 "I'VE BEEN HERE FOR 19 YEARS, SO WEST HAM FANS ARE BORED WITH SEEING ME. IT'S LIKE MY WIFE, WHO CHANGES THE WALLPAPER EVERY THREE YEARS BECAUSE SHE GETS TIRED OF IT."

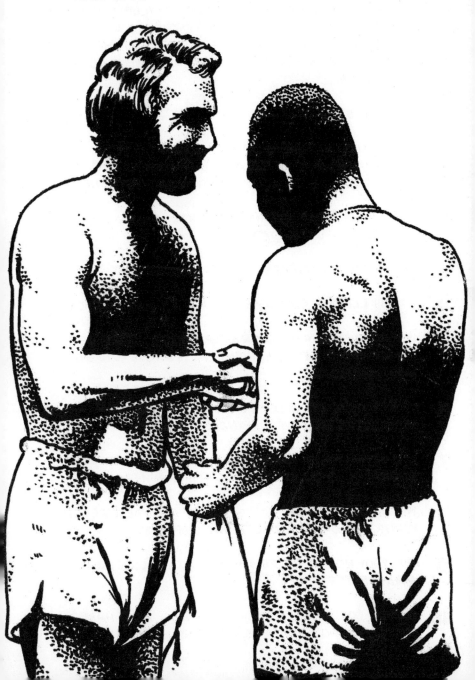

ARMBAND OF BROTHERS

JOE COLE WAS ONLY 21 YEARS OLD WHEN *GLENN ROEDER* HANDED HIM THE CAPTAIN'S ARMBAND IN JANUARY, 2003. THE YOUNGSTER'S PERFORMANCES THAT SEASON WERE STRONG ENOUGH TO WIN HIM THE HAMMER OF THE YEAR AWARD ... BUT NOT ENOUGH TO HELP THE CLUB AVOID RELEGATION FROM THE PREMIER LEAGUE, AFTER WHICH *COLE* WAS SOLD TO *CHELSEA*.

NAME THESE *WEST HAM* CAPTAINS:

1 1957-60: FIRST *HAMMERS* CAPTAIN NOT FROM THE UNITED KINGDOM, *REPUBLIC OF IRELAND* FULL-BACK WHO WENT ON TO WIN LEAGUE AND FA CUP HONOURS WITH *MANCHESTER UNITED*.

2 1960-62: *WALES* STRIKER WHO WENT ON TO ACHIEVE MUCH SUCCESS IN THE UNITED STATES.

3 1962-74: *THE HAMMERS* RETIRED HIS NUMBER 6 SHIRT.

4 1974-84: *LONDON STADIUM* EAST STAND IS NAMED IN HIS HONOUR.

5 1984-90: 21 YEARS A *HAMMER* AFTER WHICH HE HAD A BRIEF SWANSONG WITH *LEYTON ORIENT* IN 1996 BEFORE MANAGING *SOUTHEND UNITED*.

6 1990-92: MIDFIELDER WHOSE EIGHT YEARS AT *WEST HAM* CAME IN BETWEEN TWO SPELLS WITH *MANCHESTER CITY*.

7 1992-93 AND 1996-97: HARDMAN WHO SPENT 13 MONTHS WITH *LIVERPOOL* BEFORE RETURNING TO *THE HAMMERS*.

8 1993-96: DEFENDER WHO, HAVING SPENT 17 YEARS AS A *WEST HAM* PLAYER, JOINED THE CLUB'S COACHING STAFF IN 2011.

9 1997-2001: *NORTHERN IRELAND* MIDFIELDER SIGNED FROM *MANCHESTER CITY*.

10 2001-03: CONTROVERSIAL ITALIAN MAVERICK -- *WEST HAM'S* FIRST CAPTAIN NOT FROM THE BRITISH ISLES.

11   2003-05: *SCOTLAND* CENTRE-BACK SIGNED FROM *BLACKBURN ROVERS*.

12   2005-07: MIDFIELDER WHO WAS TRANSFERRED TO *ASTON VILLA* FOR £8,5 MILLION.

13   2007-09: *AUSTRALIA* INTERNATIONAL, THE CLUB'S FIRST CAPTAIN FROM OUTSIDE EUROPE.

14   2009-11: *ENGLAND* CENTRE-BACK WHO WAS SIGNED FROM *BIRMINGHAM CITY*.

15   2011-15: MIDFIELDER WHO WON PROMOTIONS WITH *BOLTON WANDERERS, NEWCASTLE UNITED* AND *THE HAMMERS*, APPOINTED *WEST HAM* ASSISTANT MANAGER IN 2019.

AFRICA CUP OF NATIONS

HAVING REPRESENTED **ALGERIA** AT THE AFRICA CUP OF NATIONS IN 2013 AND 2015 -- DURING HIS **WEST HAM** DAYS HE WAS OMITTED FROM THE 2017 SQUAD -- THE 2019 TOURNAMENT PROVED THIRD TIME LUCKY FOR WINGER **SOFIANE FEGHOULI**. HE SCORED A GOAL IN THE QUARTER-FINALS EN ROUTE TO THE FINAL, IN WHICH **ALGERIA** BEAT **SENEGAL** 1-0.

NAME THESE OTHER **WEST HAM** PLAYERS WHO HAVE COMPETED IN THE AFRICA CUP OF NATIONS:

1 CLUB RECORD SIGNING WHEN HE JOINED **WEST HAM** IN A £20.5 MILLION DEAL IN 2016, HE SCORED FOR **GHANA** AT THE 2010, 2012, 2015, 2017 AND 2019 TOURNAMENTS.

2 STRIKER WHO LEFT **WEST HAM** FOR **SPURS** IN 2003, HE SCORED FOUR GOALS AS **MALI** REACHED THE SEMI-FINALS OF THE 2014 TOURNAMENT, AND SCORED IN THE 2008 AND 2010 TOURNAMENTS.

3 DEFENDER WHO SPENT FOUR SEASONS AT **WEST HAM** BEFORE JOINING **CRYSTAL PALACE** IN 2018, HE CAPTAINED THE LOSING **SENEGAL** SIDE IN THE 2019 AFRICA CUP OF NATIONS FINAL.

4 **LIVERPOOL** AND **WEST HAM** DEFENDER, HE APPEARED IN A RECORD EIGHT AFRICA CUP OF NATIONS TOURNAMENTS FOR **CAMEROON**, WINNING TWICE, IN 2000 AND 2002.

5 UEFA CHAMPIONS LEAGUE WINNER WITH **PORTO** WHO PLAYED WITH **BLACKBURN ROVERS** AND **WEST HAM**. WITH **SOUTH AFRICA**, HE WAS JOINT TOP SCORER IN THE 1998 AFRICAN CUP OF NATIONS WITH SEVEN GOALS, INCLUDING FOUR IN 13 MINUTES AGAINST **NAMIBIA**. HE WAS ALSO NAMED PLAYER OF THE TOURNAMENT.

6 **NIGERIA** STRIKER WHO PLAYED ON LOAN AT **WEST HAM** IN 2016, HE WAS TOP SCORER IN THE 2013 TOURNAMENT, BUT MISSED THE VICTORY IN THE FINAL BECAUSE OF A THIGH INJURY.

7 PREMIER LEAGUE WINNER WITH **CHELSEA**, WHOSE CLUBS INCLUDE **LIVERPOOL**, **STOKE**, **WEST HAM** AND **SPARTAK MOSCOW**, A FORMER **ENGLAND** YOUTH AND U-21 PLAYER WHO WON THE AFRICA CUP OF NATIONS TOURNAMENT WITH **NIGERIA** IN 2013.

CAMPEONES

CARLOS TEVEZ WON LEAGUE TITLES WITH **BOCA JUNIORS** IN ARGENTINA, WITH **CORINTHIANS** IN BRAZIL, WITH BOTH **MANCHESTER UNITED** AND **MANCHESTER CITY** AND IN ITALY WITH **JUVENTUS**.

IDENTIFY THESE **WEST HAM** PLAYERS WHO WON LEAGUE TITLES IN MORE THAN ONE COUNTRY:

1 **PARIS SAINT-GERMAIN:** 2012-13, 2017-18, 2018-19
    REAL MADRID: 2019-20

2 **RIVER PLATE:** 2003-04
    CORINTHIANS: 2005
    BARCELONA: 2010-11, 2012-13, 2014-15, 2015-16, 2017-18

3 **PORTO:** 1984-85, 1985-86
    AC MILAN: 1995-96

4 **AJAX:** 1997-98
    PORTO: 2003-04, 2005-06
    ORLANDO PIRATES: 2011-12

5 **GUADALAJARA:** 2006
    MANCHESTER UNITED: 2010-11, 2012-13

6 **HAJDUK SPLIT:** 2003-04
    RANGERS: 2010-11

NATIONAL HEROES

AMONG THE INDIVIDUAL HONOURS THAT **DAVOR ŠUKER** WON DURING HIS CAREER WERE THE GOLDEN BOOT AND SILVER BALL AT THE 1998 WORLD CUP, THE GOLDEN BALL AND THE GOLDEN PLAYER AT THE 1990 UEFA EUROPEAN UNDER-21 CHAMPIONSHIP AND THE ONZE DE BRONZE. HE WAS ALSO NAMED CROATIAN FOOTBALLER OF THE YEAR SIX TIMES.

NAME THE WINNERS OF THESE FOOTBALLER OF THE YEAR AWARDS:

1 AUSTRIAN FOOTBALLER OF THE YEAR: 2018

2 CZECH FOOTBALLER OF THE YEAR: 2019, 2020

3 POLISH FOOTBALLER OF THE YEAR: 2018

4 AFRICAN FOOTBALLER OF THE YEAR: 2007

5 SOUTH AMERICAN FOOTBALLER OF THE YEAR: 2003, 2004, 2005

6 GULDBOLLEN (SWEDEN): 2002, 2006

7 KNIKSEN OF THE YEAR (NORWAY): 2005, 2007, 2008

8 CONCACAF MEN'S PLAYER OF THE YEAR: 2015

9 PORTUGUESE FOOTBALLER OF THE YEAR: 1986, 1987

10 FAI SENIOR INTERNATIONAL PLAYER OF THE YEAR: 2010, 2013

WHERE IN THE WORLD?

SWEDEN INTERNATIONAL **FREDDIE LJUNGBERG** WON HONOURS WITH **HALMSTAD** IN SWEDEN, IN ENGLAND WITH **ARSENAL** AND IN THE STATES WITH THE **SEATTLE SOUNDERS**. IN A CAREER THAT ALSO SAW HIM PLAY A SEASON WITH **WEST HAM**, HE SPENT TIME IN SCOTLAND WITH **CELTIC,** JAPAN WITH **SHIMIZU S-PULSE** AND INDIA WITH **MUMBAI CITY.**

IN WHICH COUNTRY DID THE FOLLOWING **HAMMERS** PLAY FOR THE TEAMS LISTED BELOW?

1 TONY COTTEE -- SELANGOR

2 ANTON FERDINAND -- POLICE UNITED

3 PERRY SUCKLING -- ERNEST BOREL

4 CARLTON COLE -- PERSIB BANDUNG

5 ALEX SONG -- ARTA/SOLAR7

6 JLLOYD SAMUEL -- ESTEGHLAL

7 ROBBIE KEANE -- ATK

8 BILLY MEHMET -- TAMPINES ROVERS

9 TREVOR BROOKING -- MANUREWA

10 BOBBY MOORE -- INGLEWOOD KIEV

RED DRAGONS

ARGENTINA STARS **CARLOS TEVEZ** AND **JAVIER MASCHERANO** ARRIVED AT **WEST HAM** FROM BRAZIL'S **CORINTHIANS** IN THE SUMMER OF 2006 IN A DEAL THAT WAS SHROUDED IN MYSTERY AND CONCERNS ABOUT THIRD-PARTY OWNERSHIP. **MASCHERANO'S** STAY AT UPTON PARK WAS BRIEF AND UNHAPPY AND BY FEBRUARY OF 2007 HE WAS A **LIVERPOOL** PLAYER. IN 2010, HE MOVED TO **BARCELONA**, WHERE HIS HONOURS INCLUDED TWO UEFA CHAMPIONS LEAGUES AND FIVE LEAGUE TITLES. CAPPED 147 TIMES BY HIS COUNTRY, HE JOINED CHINESE SUPER LEAGUE SIDE **HEBEI CHINA FORTUNE** IN 2018, BEFORE ENDING HIS PLAYING CAREER BACK IN ARGENTINA WITH **ESTUDIANTES**.

NAME THESE OTHER **HAMMERS** WHO'VE PLAYED OR MANAGED IN CHINA:

1 WHICH **SENEGAL** STRIKER, WHOSE CLUBS INCLUDED **WEST HAM**, **NEWCASTLE UNITED** AND **CHELSEA**, A SÜPER LIG WINNER WITH TWO DIFFERENT TURKISH CLUBS, HAD TWO SPELLS WITH **SHANGHAI SHENHUA**?

2 WHICH *CROATIA* STRIKER, WHO JOINED *WEST HAM* IN 2015 AFTER PLAYING WITH *RANGERS, EVERTON* AND *HULL CITY*, SPENT TIME IN CHINA WITH *BEIJING RENHE* AND *GUIZHOU ZHICHENG*?

3 BEFORE TAKING THE REINS AT *WEST HAM*, WHICH MANAGER HAD SPENT TWO YEARS IN CHARGE OF *HEBEI CHINA FORTUNE*?

4 WHICH FORMER *WEST HAM* PLAYER AND MANAGER WAS APPOINTED MANAGER OF *BEIJING GUOAN* IN 2021?

5 WHICH PORTUGUESE FORWARD, WHOSE WINNING GOAL CLINCHED PROMOTION IN 2012 FOR *THE HAMMERS* IN HIS DEBUT SEASON, LATER PLAYED WITH *HENAN JIANYE* AND *QINGDAO HUANGHAI*?

6 WHICH *AUSTRIA* FORWARD, A *HAMMER OF THE YEAR* WINNER, LEFT FOR *SHANGHAI PORT* IN A £22.4 MILLION DEAL IN 2019?

SLAYING RED DEVILS

DESPITE BEING USED PRIMARILY AS A SUBSTITUTE BY *GLENN ROEDER*, *JERMAIN DEFOE* WAS *WEST HAM'S* TOP SCORER IN THE 2001-02 SEASON -- HIS FIRST FULL SEASON AT *UPTON PARK* AFTER SPENDING MUCH OF THE PREVIOUS TERM ON LOAN WITH *BOURNEMOUTH.* HE HIT 14 GOALS IN 39 LEAGUE AND CUP GAMES, ONE OF WHICH WAS A 1-0 AWAY WIN AGAINST *MANCHESTER UNITED*, THE FIRST TIME THEY HAD LEFT *OLD TRAFFORD* WITH ALL THE POINTS IN 15 YEARS! *THE HAMMERS* FINISHED SEVENTH IN THE PREMIER LEAGUE THAT SEASON.

WEST HAM WON AT **OLD TRAFFORD** JUST SIX TIMES PRIOR TO THE SECOND WORLD WAR. CAN YOU IDENTIFY THE SCORERS IN THESE POST-WAR GAMES THAT SAW **THE HAMMERS** BEAT **UNITED** IN FRONT OF THE **STRETFORD END?**

1 1961 -- DIVISION ONE: TWO GOALS FROM WHICH SCOTTISH INSIDE-LEFT, THE JOINT THIRD MOST PROLIFIC SCORER IN CLUB HISTORY, GAVE **THE HAMMERS** A 2-0 VICTORY?

2 1963 -- DIVISION ONE: A SINGLE GOAL FROM WHICH YOUNG CENTRE-FORWARD WAS ENOUGH TO SETTLE THE GAME? LATER IN THE SEASON, THE PLAYER SUFFERED A SERIOUS KNEE INJURY THAT DOGGED HIM FOR THE REST OF HIS **WEST HAM** CAREER. AFTER SIGNING FOR **BLACKBURN ROVERS** IN 1967, AN EXPLORATORY OPERATION REVEALED A BROKEN KNEECAP. HIS CAREER WAS OVER AT THE AGE OF 21 AND **THE HAMMERS** WERE OBLIGED TO RETURN SOME OF THE £25,000 TRANSFER FEE.

3 1976 -- DIVISION ONE: GOALS FROM WHICH FORMER **WATFORD** STRIKER AND WHICH **ENGLAND** MIDFIELDER GAVE THE VISITORS A 2-0 WIN?

4 1986 -- FA CUP: HAVING DRAWN 1-1 AT **THE BOLEYN GROUND**, **THE HAMMERS** KNOCKED OUT THE DEFENDING CHAMPIONS IN THE REPLAY. GOALS FROM WHICH **SCOTLAND** DEFENDER AND WHICH SUBSEQUENT **NOTTS COUNTY** MIDFIELDER EARNING A 2-0 WIN?

5 1986 -- DIVISION ONE: TWO GOALS FROM WHICH **SCOTLAND** STRIKER AND ONE FROM **ALAN DEVONSHIRE** EARNED A 3-2 WIN?

6 2001 -- FA CUP: A GOAL FROM WHICH ITALIAN PUT **UNITED** OUT?

7 2007 -- PREMIER LEAGUE: WHO SCORED THE GOAL THAT GAVE **THE HAMMERS** THE 1-0 WIN THAT KEPT THEM IN THE TOP FLIGHT?

8 2021 -- LEAGUE CUP: A GOAL FROM WHICH **ARGENTINA** MIDFIELDER WAS ENOUGH TO GIVE **DAVID MOYES** A REVENGE WIN OVER HIS FORMER EMPLOYERS AND DUMP **THE RED DEVILS** OUT OF THE LEAGUE CUP?

INCE TO INTER

HAVING LAUNCHED HIS CAREER AT **WEST HAM** AND WON MULTIPLE HONOURS WITH **MANCHESTER UNITED**, **PAUL INCE** SIGNED FOR INTERNAZIONALE IN 1995. HE SPENT TWO SEASONS IN MILAN, DURING WHICH TIME HE HELPED **INTER** REACH THE UEFA CUP FINAL, BEFORE CUTTING SHORT HIS STAY IN SERIE A, CITING FAMILY REASONS FOR HIS RETURN TO ENGLAND. HAVING LEFT **WEST HAM** UNDER A CLOUD, HE MANAGED TO ALIENATE A SEGMENT OF THE **MANCHESTER UNITED** SUPPORT BY SIGNING FOR **LIVERPOOL**!

IDENTIFY THESE ITALIAN CONNECTIONS TO **WEST HAM UNITED**:

1 WITH WHICH CLUB DID *PAULO FUTRE* WIN A SERIE A TITLE IN 1995?

2 *ANGELO OGBONNA* WAS A £10 MILLION CAPTURE FROM WHICH SERIE A CLUB IN 2015?

3 WITH WHICH CLUB DID *PAOLO DI CANIO* WIN THE 1993 UEFA CUP?

4 WHICH *CZECH REPUBLIC* CENTRE-BACK JOINED *WEST HAM* FROM *FIORENTINA* IN 2001?

5 WHICH SPANISH-BORN *EQUATORIAL GUINEA* MIDFIELDER JOINED *WEST HAM* FROM *SAMPDORIA* IN 2015 AND RETURNED TO ITALY FOUR YEARS LATER TO PLAY FOR *SASSUOLO*?

6 AS A PLAYER, *WEST HAM* MANAGER *GIANFRANCO ZOLA* WON THE 1994 UEFA CUP WITH WHICH ITALIAN TEAM?

7 WHICH BRAZILIAN MIDFIELDER, A £36 MILLION SIGNING FROM *LAZIO* IN 2018, RETURNED TO THE CLUB IN 2021 AFTER THREE SEASONS WITH *WEST HAM*?

8 FROM WHICH ITALIAN CLUB DID *GERMANY* INTERNATIONAL *THOMAS HITZLSPERGER* ARRIVE AT *WEST HAM* IN 2010?

9 WHICH *ITALY* INTERNATIONAL, CAPPED 17 TIMES BY THE *AZZURRI*, WHO SPENT THE 2009-10 SEASON WITH *WEST HAM*, PLAYED FOR 10 DIFFERENT TEAMS IN ITALY -- INCLUDING *FIORENTINA* AND *ATALANTA* -- AS WELL AS CLUBS IN CHINA AND AUSTRALIA?

10 WHICH *SWITZERLAND* INTERNATIONAL MIDFIELDER, BORN IN KOSOVO, JOINED *WEST HAM* FROM *LAZIO* IN 2008 AND SPENT THREE SEASONS WITH *THE HAMMERS* BEFORE SIGNING FOR *FIORENTINA*? HIS SUBSEQUENT CLUBS INCLUDE *NAPOLI*, *HAMBURGER SV*, *WATFORD*, *UDINESE* AND *SION*, BEFORE HE JOINED *GENOA* IN 2020.

GREENWOOD THE GREAT

IN HIS 13 YEARS AS **WEST HAM** MANAGER, **RON GREENWOOD** WON THE FA CUP IN 1964 AND THE EUROPEAN CUP WINNERS' CUP IN 1965 -- THE FIRST TWO MAJOR TROPHIES IN THE CLUB'S HISTORY. HE ALSO BROUGHT THROUGH SOME INCREDIBLE HOMEGROWN TALENT, INCLUDING WORLD CUP-WINNERS **BOBBY MOORE, GEOFF HURST** AND **MARTIN PETERS.**

GREENWOOD SIGNED THESE PLAYERS FROM WHICH CLUBS?

1   *GRAHAM PADDON*

2   *POP ROBSON*

3   *PETER EUSTACE*

4   *ALAN STEPHENSON*

5   *BOBBY FERGUSON*

6   *JOHNNY BYRNE*

7   *BILLY BONDS*

8   *PETER BRABROOK*

9   *JIMMY GREAVES*

10   *TED MACDOUGALL*

11 *JIM STANDEN*

12 *BRIAN DEAR*

13 *MICK MCGIVEN*

14 *LAWRIE LESLIE*

15 *BERTIE LUTTON*

16 *JOHN CUSHLEY*

17 *DUDLEY TYLER*

18 *KEITH COLEMAN*

THE BOYS OF 1994

adidas

11

HAVING EARNED MULTIPLE HONOURS WITH *STEAUA BUCUREŞTI*, *ILIE DUMITRESCU* WAS A MAJOR PART OF *ROMANIA'S* SUCCESS AT THE 1994 WORLD CUP, HIS TWO GOALS AND ONE ASSIST HELPING BEAT *ARGENTINA* 3-2 TO TAKE HIS COUNTRY TO THE QUARTER-FINALS FOR THE FIRST TIME IN THEIR WORLD CUP HISTORY. HE SUBSEQUENTLY PLAYED FOR *SPURS* AND *WEST HAM* BEFORE HEADING TO MEXICO.

IDENTIFY THESE OTHER PAST, PRESENT OR FUTURE *HAMMERS* WHO REPRESENTED THEIR COUNTRIES AT THE 1994 WORLD CUP:

1 *ROMANIA*: STRIKER PLAYING WITH *AC MILAN* AT THE TIME.

2 *USA*: MIDFIELDER PLAYING WITH *DERBY COUNTY* AT THE TIME.

3 *CAMEROON* (2): DEFENDER WHO WOULD WIN THE UEFA CUP WITH *LIVERPOOL* AND A MIDFIELDER WHO WOULD DIE ONFIELD AGED 28.

4 *REPUBLIC OF IRELAND* (2): MIDFIELDER PLAYING WITH *ASTON VILLA* AT THE TIME AND A FORMER *WEST HAM* FORWARD WHO WAS PLAYING FOR *WOLVERHAMPTON WANDERERS*.

ANY OLD IRONS

NIGEL WINTERBURN CALLED TIME ON A CAREER THAT BROUGHT HIM TWO **ENGLAND** CAPS AND A MULTITUDE OF HONOURS WITH **ARSENAL** WHEN HE PLAYED FOR **WEST HAM** AGAINST **LIVERPOOL** IN FEBRUARY 2003 AT THE AGE OF 39 YEARS AND 53 DAYS.

IDENTIFY THESE OTHER *WEST HAM* VETERANS:

1 *FINLAND* GOALKEEPER WHO MADE HIS FINAL APPEARANCE FOR *WEST HAM* IN 2003 WHEN HE WAS APPROACHING 40, BEFORE GOING ON TO JOIN *WIGAN ATHLETIC* AND THEN END HIS CAREER IN THE INDIAN SUPER LEAGUE AT THE AGE OF 42.

2 CENTRE-BACK WHO WON THE FA CUP IN 1980, HE ENDED HIS TWO-DECADE SERVICE TO *WEST HAM* PLAYING IN A 1-1 DRAW WITH *SHEFFIELD WEDNESDAY* IN 1996, AT THE AGE OF 37 YEARS AND 280 DAYS, BEFORE EXTENDING HIS CAREER WITH *LEYTON ORIENT.*

3 FORWARD WHO BECAME *WEST HAM'S* OLDEST PREMIER LEAGUE PLAYER WHEN HE PLAYED AGAINST *MANCHESTER CITY* IN 2006 AT THE AGE OF 40 YEARS AND 272 DAYS OLD. AN *ENGLAND* INTERNATIONAL, HE WAS 42 AND PLAYING FOR *COLCHESTER UNITED* WHEN HE FINALLY RETIRED.

4 AT 41 YEARS AND 226 DAYS OLD, *WEST HAM'S* OLDEST-EVER PLAYER WHEN HE APPEARED AGAINST *SOUTHAMPTON* IN 1988.

5 FORMER *MANCHESTER UNITED* GOALKEEPER WHO MADE HIS FINAL *WEST HAM* APPEARANCE IN 1997, A FEW MONTHS SHY OF HIS 40TH BIRTHDAY, COINCIDENTALLY AGAINST *UNITED*. HE REMAINED ON THE *WEST HAM* BOOKS UNTIL HE WAS 42, WHEN HE RETIRED TO TAKE UP A POSITION WITH THE CLUB AS A COACH. TRAGICALLY, HE DIED OF A HEART ATTACK THE FOLLOWING YEAR.

6 FIERCE *ENGLAND* DEFENDER, WHO HAD WON HONOURS WITH *NOTTINGHAM FOREST* AND *MANCHESTER CITY*, HE WAS 39 YEARS AND 27 DAYS OLD WHEN HE MADE HIS FINAL APPEARANCE FOR *WEST HAM* IN 2001, THE SAME SEASON HE WAS VOTED *HAMMER OF THE YEAR.*

7 GOALKEEPER WHO PLAYED MORE THAN 400 TIMES FOR *QUEENS PARK RANGERS* BEFORE MAKING MORE THAN 400 APPEARANCES FOR *WEST HAM*. HE LEFT *THE HAMMERS* WEEKS BEFORE HIS 40TH BIRTHDAY TO LINK UP FOR A SWANSONG AT *IPSWICH TOWN* UNDER *JOHN LYALL.*

BLUE MEN GROUP

JOE COLE ONCE SCORED SEVEN GOALS FOR THE *ENGLAND* YOUTH TEAM IN A GAME AGAINST *SPAIN*. HE MADE HIS SENIOR DEBUT FOR *WEST HAM* AT THE AGE OF 17, AND WAS GIVEN THE CAPTAIN'S ARMBAND AT THE AGE OF 21. FOLLOWING *WEST HAM'S* 2003 RELEGATION -- THE SAME SEASON HE WAS VOTED *HAMMER OF THE YEAR* -- HE WAS SOLD TO *CHELSEA* IN A £6 MILLION DEAL. HE WON THREE LEAGUE TITLES, TWO FA CUPS AND THE LEAGUE CUP WITH *"THE PENSIONERS"* BEFORE JOINING *LIVERPOOL* IN 2010.

NAME THESE OTHER *WEST HAM* AND *CHELSEA* PLAYERS:

1 RIGHT-BACK CAPPED 54 TIMES BY *ENGLAND*, AFTER LEAVING *WEST HAM* HE WON THE PREMIER LEAGUE AND LEAGUE CUP IN 2005 WITH *CHELSEA*, THE 2008 FA CUP WITH *PORTSMOUTH* AND THE 2011 LEAGUE CUP WITH *LIVERPOOL*, BEFORE ENDING HIS PLAYING CAREER WITH THREE SEASONS AT *STOKE CITY*.

2 CAPPED 102 TIMES BY *ISRAEL*, DURING HIS TIME IN ENGLISH FOOTBALL HE PLAYED FOR *WEST HAM, LIVERPOOL, CHELSEA, ARSENAL* AND *QUEENS PARK RANGERS*.

3 SCORER OF 10 GOALS IN A MATCH FOR *LUTON TOWN* AGAINST *BRISTOL ROVERS* IN 1936, WINGER WHO PLAYED FOR *CHELSEA* BEFORE THE SECOND WORLD WAR AND FOR *WEST HAM* AFTER.

4 CAPPED 37 TIMES BY *NIGERIA*, HIS PLAYING CAREER HAS TAKEN HIM FROM *CRYSTAL PALACE* TO *WIGAN ATHLETIC, CHELSEA, LIVERPOOL, STOKE CITY* AND *WEST HAM* AND CLUBS IN TURKEY, ITALY AND RUSSIA.

5   FORMER *CHELSEA* STRIKER, WHO SPENT LOAN PERIODS AT *WOLVES*, *CHARLTON ATHLETIC* AND *ASTON VILLA*, AND NINE SEASONS AT *WEST HAM* BEFORE JOINING *CELTIC* IN 2015.

6   AFTER EIGHT YEARS AT *CHELSEA*, WINGER WHO JOINED *WEST HAM* IN 1962 AND WON THE FA CUP TWO YEARS LATER. CAPPED THREE TIMES BY *ENGLAND*, HE JOINED *LEYTON ORIENT* IN 1968. HE WAS LATER AN ACADEMY COACH AT *WEST HAM*.

THE BIG BOSSES

RIO FERDINAND MADE 81 APPEARANCES FOR *ENGLAND* BETWEEN 1997 AND 2011. DURING THAT TIME, HE PLAYED UNDER SEVEN DIFFERENT MANAGERS: *SVEN-GÖRAN ERIKSSON, FABIO CAPELLO, STEVE MCCLAREN, GLENN HODDLE, KEVIN KEEGAN, HOWARD WILKINSON* AND *PETER TAYLOR.*

MATCH THE *WEST HAM* PLAYER TO THE MANAGERS THEY PLAYED FOR AT INTERNATIONAL LEVEL:

1 *JAVIER MASCHERANO*

2 *JAVIER HERNÁNDEZ*

3 *ROBBIE KEANE*

4 *RĂZVAN RAŢ*

5 *NICLAS ALEXANDERSSON*

6 *PAULO FUTRE*

7 *BOBBY MOORE*

8 *YOSSI BENAYOUN*

9 *RIGOBERT SONG*

10 *PETER SHILTON*

11 *ILIE DUMITRESCU*

12 *DEMBA BA*

13 *JOHN HARKES*

14 *LUCAS NEILL*

15 *CRAIG BELLAMY*

16 *JOHN CAREW*

17 *IGOR ŠTIMAC*

18 *BENNI MCCARTHY*

19 *IAIN DOWIE*

20 *EMMANUEL EMENIKE*

A: CAMEROON ARIE HAAN, OTTO PFISTER, WINFRIED SCHÄFER, PAUL LE GUEN, HENRI MICHEL, ARTUR JORGE, CLAUDE LE ROY, PIERRE LECHANTRE, ROBERT CORFOU

B: AUSTRALIA *HOLGER OSIEK, GUUS HIDDINK, PIM VERBEEK, TERRY VENABLES, FRANK FARINA, GRAHAM ARNOLD, AURELIO VIDMAR, ANGE POSTECOGLOU, RAÚL BLANCO*

C: ARGENTINA JOSÉ NÉSTOR PEKERMAN, MARCELO BIELSA, ALFIO BASILE, TATA MARTINO, SERGIO BATISTA, EDGARDO BAUZA, DIEGO MARADONA, ALEJANDRO SABELLA

D: MEXICO *JAVIER AGUIRRE, LUIS FERNANDO TENA, RICARDO FERRETTI, ENRIQUE MEZA, VICTOR VUCETICH, JOSÉ MANUEL DE LA TORRE, EFRAÍN FLORES, TATA MARTINO, MIGUEL HERRERA*

E: NIGERIA STEPHEN KESHI, AUGUSTINE EGUAVOEN, SUNDAY OLISEH, SAMSON SIASIA, SHAIBU AMODU

F: NORWAY *AGE HAREIDE, EGIL OLSEN, NILS JOHAN SEMB*

G: SWEDEN LARS LAGERBÄCK, TOMMY SÖDERBERG, TOMMY SVENSSON

H: SENEGAL *ALAIN GIRESSE, HENRYK KASPERCZAK, LAMINE NDIAYE, AMARA TRAORÉ, PAOLO BERRETTINI, ALIOU CISSÉ, JOSEPH KOTO*

I: SOUTH AFRICA CARLOS QUEIROZ, PHILIPPE TROUSSIER, STUART BAXTER, CARLOS ALBERTO PARREIRA, TED DUMITRU, JOEL SANTANA, CLIVE BARKER, GORDON IGESUND, STEVE KOMPHELA

J: PORTUGAL *CARLOS QUEIROZ, NELO VINGADA, ARTUR JORGE, JOSÉ TORRES, FERNANDO CABRITA, ANTÓNIO OLIVEIRA, RUY SEABRA, JUCA*

K: ENGLAND ALF RAMSEY, WALTER WINTERBOTTOM

L: ISRAEL *LUIS FERNANDEZ, DROR KASHTAN, AVRAM GRANT, ELI GUTTMAN, RICHARD MØLLER NIELSEN, ELISHA LEVY, SHLOMO SCHARF, ELI OHANA, ALON HAZAN*

M: REPUBLIC OF IRELAND MARTIN O'NEILL, GIOVANNI TRAPATTONI, MICK MCCARTHY, BRIAN KERR, STEVE STAUNTON, DON GIVENS, NOEL KING

N: ENGLAND *SIR BOBBY ROBSON, RON GREENWOOD, ALF RAMSEY, DON REVIE, JOE MERCER*

O: ROMANIA GHEORGHE HAGI, ANGHEL IORDANESCU, VICTOR PITURCA, EMERICH JENEI, GHEORGHE CONSTANTIN, CORNEL DINU, MIRCEA RADULESCU

P: UNITED STATES *BORA MILUTINOVIĆ, BRUCE ARENA, BOB GANSLER, STEVE SAMPSON, SIGI SCHMID, GORAN MILUTINOVIC, JOHN KOWALSKI*

Q: CROATIA MIROSLAV BLAŽEVIĆ, STANKO POKLEPOVIĆ, MIRKO JOZIĆ, DRAŽAN JERKOVIĆ

R: NORTHERN IRELAND *BILLY BINGHAM, LAWRIE MCMENEMY, BRYAN HAMILTON*

S: ROMANIA ANGHEL IORDANESCU, RAZVAN LUCESCU, VICTOR PITURCA, EMIL SANDOI

T: WALES *CHRIS COLEMAN, MARK HUGHES, JOHN TOSHACK, GARY SPEED, BRIAN FLYNN, BOB GOULD*

MEET THE NEW BOSS, SAME AS THE OLD BOSS ...

JERMAIN DEFOE PLAYED UNDER **HARRY REDKNAPP** AT THREE DIFFERENT CLUBS -- **WEST HAM, PORTSMOUTH** AND **SPURS.**

UNDER WHICH **WEST HAM** MANAGER DID THESE **HAMMERS** PLAY AT MULTIPLE CLUBS:

1   **ABDOULAYE FAYÉ: BOLTON WANDERERS, NEWCASTLE UNITED** AND **WEST HAM**

2   **GÖKHAN TÖRE: BEŞIKTAŞ** AND **WEST HAM**

3   **JONATHAN SPECTOR: WEST HAM** AND **BIRMINGHAM CITY**

4   **RIO FERDINAND: QUEENS PARK RANGERS** AND **WEST HAM**

5   **WAYNE BRIDGE: CHELSEA** AND **WEST HAM**

6   **PAUL GODDARD: WEST HAM** AND **IPSWICH TOWN**

7   **JAMES TOMKINS: WEST HAM** AND **CRYSTAL PALACE**

8   **LUKE CHADWICK: READING** AND **WEST HAM**

9   **LEE BOWYER: CHARLTON ATHLETIC** AND **WEST HAM**

10   **LEE BOWYER: NEWCASTLE UNITED** AND **WEST HAM**

11   **PATRICE EVRA: MANCHESTER UNITED** AND **WEST HAM**

12   **ANDY CARROLL: NEWCASTLE UNITED** AND **WEST HAM**

13   **FRÉDÉRIC PIQUIONNE: PORTSMOUTH** AND **WEST HAM**

CLARET AND BLUE DRAGONS

2009 SAW **MAROUANE CHAMAKH** WIN THE **MARC-VIVIEN FOÉ AWARD**, GIVEN TO THE BEST PLAYER WHO REPRESENTS AN AFRICAN NATIONAL FOOTBALL TEAM IN LIGUE 1, IN A YEAR THAT SAW HIM WIN A TREBLE OF LEAGUE, LEAGUE CUP AND TROPHÉE DES CHAMPIONS WITH **BORDEAUX**. HAVING JOINED **ARSENAL** ON A FREE TRANSFER IN 2010, HE WAS LOANED OUT TO **WEST HAM** IN 2013, BEFORE MOVING ON TO **CRYSTAL PALACE** LATER THAT YEAR.

CHAMAKH ENDED HIS PLAYING DAYS WITH A BRIEF SPELL AT **CARDIFF CITY** IN 2018. IDENTIFY THESE OTHER **WEST HAM** PLAYERS WHO ALSO JOINED CLUBS BASED IN WALES:

1 GOALKEEPER WHO WON A LEAGUE TITLE WITH **LEGIA WARSAW**, THE 2014 FA CUP WITH **ARSENAL** AND SPENT FOUR SEASONS WITH **SWANSEA CITY**.

2 **MANCHESTER UNITED** PRODIGY WHO JOINED **DERBY COUNTY** IN 2021 AFTER PLAYING FOR A SUCCESSION OF CLUBS, INCLUDING **WEST HAM**, **BIRMINGHAM CITY**, **CARDIFF CITY**, **QPR** AND TEAMS IN ITALY, SWEDEN, MEXICO AND THE NETHERLANDS.

3 HAVING EARNED PROMOTION TO THE SECOND TIER WITH **CARDIFF CITY** IN 2003, DEFENDER WHO JOINED **WEST HAM** IN 2005. HE SPENT SIX YEARS AT THE CLUB, BEFORE MOVING ON TO **QPR** AND **CRYSTAL PALACE**, FINALLY RETURNING TO **CARDIFF** IN 2014.

4 STRIKER WHO LAUNCHED HIS CAREER AT **WEST HAM**, WHERE HE WAS LOANED OUT TO SEVEN CLUBS -- INCLUDING **SWANSEA CITY** -- BEFORE JOINING **WOLVES** IN 2012. HIS LENGTHY LIST OF SUBSEQUENT CLUBS INCLUDE **IPSWICH TOWN, NEWPORT COUNTY** AND **COLCHESTER UNITED**, AS WELL AS TEAMS IN CHINA.

5 *ENGLAND* INTERNATIONAL WHOSE STELLAR CAREER INCLUDED A MID-1990S LOAN SPELL WITH *SWANSEA CITY* WHEN HE WAS FIRST BREAKING THROUGH AT *WEST HAM*.

6 STRIKER SIGNED TO *WEST HAM* FROM *BRISTOL CITY* IN EARLY 2012, HE WON PROMOTION TO THE TOP FLIGHT IN HIS BRIEF STAY AT THE CLUB, BEFORE JOINING *CARDIFF CITY* LATER THAT YEAR.

7 *GHANA* INTERNATIONAL WINGER WHOSE TWO SPELLS AT *CARDIFF CITY* CAME EITHER SIDE OF A £20.5 MILLION MOVE TO *WEST HAM* IN 2016 THAT LASTED LESS THAN 18 MONTHS.

8 *WALES* INTERNATIONAL CENTRE-BACK SIGNED TO *WEST HAM* FROM *CARDIFF CITY* IN 2005, HE HAD THREE YEARS AT *ASTON VILLA* BEFORE RETURNING TO *THE HAMMERS* IN 2012 AND SPENDING ANOTHER SIX SEASONS AT THE CLUB.

9 HAVING WON HONOURS WITH *CELTIC* AND *LIVERPOOL* IN A CAREER THAT TOOK HIM TO CLUBS INCLUDING *BLACKBURN ROVERS*, *WEST HAM* AND *MANCHESTER CITY*, *WALES* INTERNATIONAL WHO ENDED HIS PLAYING CAREER AT *CARDIFF CITY*, HELPING THE CLUB GAIN PROMOTION TO THE TOP FLIGHT IN 2013.

AVRAM'S ADDITIONS

FOLLOWING A SUCCESSFUL LOAN AT *CELTIC*, *ROBBIE KEANE* JOINED *WEST HAM* ON LOAN FROM *TOTTENHAM HOTSPUR* IN EARLY 2011. *THE HAMMERS* HAD AN OPTION TO EXTEND THE DEAL BY TWO YEARS IF THEY AVOIDED RELEGATION FROM THE PREMIER LEAGUE -- HOWEVER, THEY COULDN'T AVOID THE DROP AND THE *REPUBLIC OF IRELAND* STRIKER RETURNED TO *TOTTENHAM*.

THE RELEGATION BROUGHT TO AN END THE ONE-SEASON TENURE OF *AVRAM GRANT* AS MANAGER. IDENTIFY THESE OTHER *AVRAM* ACQUISITIONS BY THE CLUB FROM WHICH THEY ARRIVED:

1 RIGHT-WINGER FROM MEXICO'S *UNAM*

2 NEW ZEALAND DEFENDER FROM *MIDTJYLLAND*

3 MIDFIELDER FROM *MIDDLESBROUGH*

4 *MARTINIQUE* STRIKER FROM *LYON*

5 *ENGLAND* LEFT-BACK ON LOAN FROM *MANCHESTER CITY*

6 BELGIAN GOALKEEPER FROM *MVV MAASTRICHT*

7 *GERMANY* MIDFIELDER FROM *LAZIO*

8 *ISRAEL* CENTRE-BACK ON LOAN FROM *PORTSMOUTH*

9 *DENMARK* RIGHT-BACK FROM *BLACKBURN ROVERS*

10 *NIGERIA* STRIKER ON LOAN FROM *INTERNAZIONALE*

THE BOYS IN GREEN

RAY HOUGHTON PROGRESSED THROUGH THE RANKS AT **WEST HAM** BUT, HAVING FAILED TO BREAK INTO THE FIRST TEAM, SIGNED FOR **FULHAM** IN 1982. THREE YEARS LATER HE MOVED ON TO **OXFORD UNITED**, WITH WHOM HE WON THE LEAGUE CUP IN 1986. FOUR SEASONS WITH **LIVERPOOL** BROUGHT TWO LEAGUE TITLES AND TWO FA CUPS, BEFORE HE JOINED **ASTON VILLA** IN 1992. HE WON THE LEAGUE CUP TWO YEARS LATER, BEFORE GOING ON TO PLAY FOR **CRYSTAL PALACE** AND **READING**. HE ENDED HIS PLAYING DAYS WITH A SPELL AT NON-LEAGUE **STEVENAGE BOROUGH**.

HOUGHTON WAS CAPPED 73 TIMES BY THE **REPUBLIC OF IRELAND**. IDENTIFY THESE OTHER **HAMMERS** WHO PLAYED FOR THE **REPUBLIC**:

1 CENTRE-BACK WHO MADE 63 APPEARANCES FOR THE **REPUBLIC**, HE PLAYED WITH 10 CLUBS, MOST NOTABLY **COVENTRY CITY**. FOLLOWING THE 2002 WORLD CUP HE WAS SIGNED TO **WEST HAM** ON A FREE TRANSFER. FOLLOWING RELEGATION HE MOVED ON TO **SUNDERLAND** AND **WOLVES**, PLAYING AT BOTH CLUBS UNDER HIS FORMER NATIONAL TEAM BOSS **MICK MCCARTHY**.

2 CAPPED 72 TIMES BETWEEN 1974 AND 1990, MIDFIELDER WHOSE CLUBS INCLUDED **ARSENAL, JUVENTUS, SAMPDORIA, INTERNAZIONALE, ASCOLI** AND **WEST HAM**.

3 GOALKEEPER WHO JOINED THE **HAMMERS** FROM **MIDDLESBROUGH** IN 2020, HIS SECOND SPELL WITH **WEST HAM**.

4 JOURNEYMAN STRIKER WHO WON HONOURS WITH **WALSALL, NEWCASTLE UNITED, SUNDERLAND, TRANMERE ROVERS** AND **DERRY CITY**, HE SPENT TWO SEASONS WITH **WEST HAM** AND WAS A MEMBER OF THE TEAM THAT WAS RELEGATED IN 1989.

5 STRIKER WHO WON HONOURS WITH **SUNDERLAND** AND **SOUTHAMPTON**, HIS OTHER CLUBS INCLUDED **WATFORD, FEYENOORD, LEICESTER CITY, WIGAN ATHLETIC** AND **PORTSMOUTH**. CAPPED 41 TIMES, HE PLAYED FOR **WEST HAM** IN THE 2003-04 SEASON.

GOALGETTER GLORY

THE 1980 FA CUP FINAL PITTED
SECOND-TIER SIDE **WEST HAM**
AGAINST TOP FLIGHT **ARSENAL**.
A 13TH MINUTE GOAL FROM
TREVOR BROOKING -- HE
SCORED WITH A RARE HEADER --
WAS ENOUGH TO BEAT **ARSENAL**
AND WIN THE CUP FOR **THE
HAMMERS**. TO DATE, IT IS THE
LAST TIME A TEAM FROM OUTSIDE
THE TOP FLIGHT HAS WON THE FA CUP.

WHO SCORED FOR **WEST HAM** IN THE FOLLOWING FINALS?

1   1964 FA CUP: BEAT **PRESTON NORTH END** 3-2

2   1965 EUROPEAN CUP WINNERS' CUP: BEAT **1860 MUNICH** 2-0

3   1966 LEAGUE CUP: LOST 5-3 ON AGGREGATE TO **WEST BROM**

4   1975 FA CUP: BEAT **FULHAM** 2-0

5   1976 EUROPEAN CUP WINNERS' CUP: LOST 2-4 TO **ANDERLECHT**

6   1981 LEAGUE CUP: DREW WITH **LIVERPOOL** 1-1 - LOST REPLAY 2-1

7   1999: UEFA INTERTOTO CUP: BEAT **METZ** 3-2 ON AGGREGATE

8   2006 FA CUP: DREW 3-3 WITH **LIVERPOOL**, LOST ON PENALTIES

BRIGHT SPARK!

IN THE EARLY DAYS OF HIS CAREER, WHILE PLAYING SEMI-PRO WITH **WEALDSTONE UNITED**, **STUART PEARCE** WORKED AS AN ELECTRICIAN. HE WAS 21 BEFORE HE TURNED PRO WITH **COVENTRY CITY.**

PEARCE IS ONE OF A NUMBER OF **WEST HAM** PLAYERS WHO HAVE PLAYED IN THE PREMIER LEAGUE WITH AT LEAST THREE DIFFERENT CLUBS -- HE WAS ALSO WITH **NOTTINGHAM FOREST** AND **NEWCASTLE UNITED.** CAN YOU NAME THE OTHER PREMIER LEAGUE TEAMS THESE **HAMMERS** PLAYED FOR:

1 **ANTON FERDINAND** (2)

2 **JOE COLE** (3)

3 **RIO FERDINAND** (3)

4 **ROBBIE KEANE** (5)

5 **VICTOR MOSES** (4)

6 **NIGEL QUASHIE** (5)

7 **DAVID UNSWORTH** (4)

8 **MOHAMED DIAME** (2)

9 **CARLTON COLE** (3)

10 **ROB GREEN** (2)

11 **TAL BEN HAIM** (6)

12 **PAOLO DI CANIO** (2)

BAD BOYS, BAD BOYS

THE THEFT OF A £625 DIAMOND BRACELET ON THE EVE OF THE 1970
WORLD CUP SAW **ENGLAND** CAPTAIN **BOBBY MOORE** DETAINED
FOR QUESTIONING BY THE COLOMBIAN AUTHORITIES. IT TOOK THE
INTERVENTION OF BRITISH PRIME MINISTER **HAROLD WILSON** TO GET
THE **WEST HAM** STAR RELEASED AFTER FOUR DAYS OF QUESTIONING
SO HE COULD FLY TO MEXICO TO REJOIN HIS **ENGLAND** TEAMMATES.
DECADES LATER, HOME OFFICE DOCUMENTS REVEALED THAT THE THEFT
WAS PROBABLY COMMITTED BY ANOTHER MEMBER OF THE **ENGLAND**
SQUAD, WITH **MOORE** APPARENTLY HAVING TOLD FRIENDS THAT HE
THOUGHT IT MIGHT HAVE BEEN A "PRANK GONE WRONG."

NAME AND SHAME THE FOLLOWING **WEST HAM** BAD BOYS:

1   **CZECH REPUBLIC** DEFENDER WHO EARNED TEN YELLOW CARDS
IN HIS FIRST SEASON WITH **THE IRONS** AFTER JOINING IN 2001. A
SERIES OF OFFENCES, FROM DRIVING UNDER THE INFLUENCE TO
FRAUD, SAW HIM JAILED IN HIS HOMELAND IN 2019.

2   CONTROVERSIAL ITALIAN WITH A SOFT SPOT FOR **BENITO
MUSSOLINI**, HE WAS ONCE BANNED FOR ELEVEN GAMES AND FINED
£10,000 DURING HIS **SHEFFIELD WEDNESDAY** DAYS FOR PUSHING
OVER A REFEREE.

3   FOLLOWING AN INCIDENT AT A BRENTWOOD NIGHTCLUB, WHICH
HAMMERS STAR WAS FINED £7,605 IN 2014 AFTER PLEADING
GUILTY TO ASSAULTING A POLICE CONSTABLE, BEING DRUNK AND
DISORDERLY IN A PUBLIC PLACE AND OBSTRUCTING A CONSTABLE?

4   SCOTTISH STRIKER WITH A PLAYBOY REPUTATION, WHO HAD TWO
SPELLS WITH **WEST HAM** AND TWO WITH **CELTIC** IN THE 1980S AND
1990S. HE RECEIVED A FOUR-MONTH SUSPENDED SENTENCE IN 2009
AFTER AN ALTERCATION IN DOUGLAS ON THE ISLE OF MAN IN WHICH
HE HEAD-BUTTED A MAN.

5   WHICH **WEST HAM** STRIKER WAS FINED BY THE CLUB AFTER A 1998
TRAINING ROUND INCIDENT IN WHICH HE KICKED TEAMMATE **EYAL
BERKOVIC** IN THE FACE?

6   RIGHT-WINGER WHO SPENT FIVE SEASONS WITH ***WEST HAM*** BEFORE LEAVING FOR ***MANCHESTER CITY*** IN LATE 1989, HE WAS JAILED FOR EIGHT YEARS IN 2005 FOR DRUGS OFFENCES.

7   THE OFF-FIELD MISDEMEANOURS AND DRAMAS SURROUNDING WHICH WAYWARD MIDFIELDER CONVINCED ***SIR ALEX FERGUSON*** TO ALLOW HIM TO LEAVE ***OLD TRAFFORD*** TO JOIN ***THE HAMMERS*** IN 2012 TO GET HIM AWAY FROM MANCHESTER?

GERMAN IMPORTS

A PROFESSIONAL FROM THE AGE OF 15, *JAVIER HERNÁNDEZ* EARNED THE NICKNAME *"CHICHARITO"* BECAUSE HIS FATHER, WHO WAS A MEMBER OF THE *MEXICO* 1986 WORLD CUP SQUAD, WAS NICKNAMED *"CHICHARO"* -- IT MEANS *"PEA"* IN SPANISH -- DUE TO HIS GREEN EYES. *JAVIER'S* GRANDFATHER PLAYED FOR *"EL TRICOLOR"* IN THE 1954 WORLD CUP, WHERE HE SCORED AGAINST *FRANCE.* HAVING WON HONOURS WITH *GUADALAJARA, MANCHESTER UNITED* AND *REAL MADRID,* *"CHICHARITO"* SPENT TWO SEASONS AT *BAYER LEVERKUSEN* BEFORE SIGNING FOR *WEST HAM* IN 2017.

FROM WHICH GERMAN CLUBS WERE THE FOLLOWING SIGNED ?

1 *ANDRIY YARMOLENKO*

2 *SÉBASTIEN HALLER*

3 *EMANUEL POGATETZ*

4 *HÅVARD NORDTVEIT*

5 *SLAVEN BILIĆ*

6 *DEMBA BA*

7 *DIETER ECKSTEIN*

8 *GUY DEMEL*

9 *MARC KELLER*

HAMMERS CELEBS

POP STAR **KATY PERRY'S** OUTFIT AT THE MTV EUROPE MUSIC AWARDS IN 2009 -- SHE WAS CLAD IN A **WEST HAM**-THEMED BASQUE AND PANTIES -- WAS IN HOMAGE TO HER BOYFRIEND AT THE TIME, **HAMMERS** FANATIC **RUSSELL BRAND**. THEIR SUBSEQUENT MARRIAGE LASTED A LITTLE OVER A YEAR, WHICH PRESUMABLY ALSO ENDED HER **WEST HAM** AFFINITY!

IDENTIFY THESE OTHER CELEBRITY **HAMMERS** FANS:

1 ACTOR WHOSE ROLES INCLUDE **WILL SCARLETT, BEOWULF, JACK REGAN, JIMMY ROSE, MR. BEAVER** AND **GROWLTIGER**.

2 BASSIST AND FOUNDING MEMBER OF **IRON MAIDEN**, HE SPORTS THE CLUB CREST ON HIS PRECISION BASS.

3 AKA **ELIZABETH SWANN, GUINEVERE, JULES PAXTON, DOMINO HARVEY, SABÉ** AND **ANNA KARENINA**.

4 ACTOR, WRITER AND PRODUCER WHOSE CREDITS INCLUDE **"GAVIN AND STACEY"** AND THE **"PETER RABBIT"** MOVIES.

5 SPRINT AND HURDLING TRACK AND FIELD ATHLETE WHO WON A SILVER MEDAL AT THE 1984 OLYMPICS, GOLD AT THE 1990 COMMONWEALTH GAMES AND WHOSE SUBSEQUENT CREDITS AS A TV PRESENTER INCLUDE **"RECORD BREAKERS"**.

6 **WEST HAM JUNIORS** PLAYER WHO TURNED TO ACTING AND MUSIC -- HIS MOVIE CREDITS INCLUDE **"THAT'LL BE THE DAY"** AND **"STARDUST"**, HE PLAYED EDDIE MOON ON **"EASTENDERS"** AND HIS POP HITS INCLUDE **"ROCK ON", "HOLD ME CLOSE"** AND **"GONNA MAKE YOU A STAR"**.

7 FILM DIRECTOR WHOSE CREDITS INCLUDE **"VERTIGO", "PSYCHO"** AND **"NORTH BY NORTHWEST"**.

8 **"MAMA DO (UH OH, UH OH)"** AND **"ALL ABOUT TONIGHT"** HITMAKER AND A COACH ON **"THE VOICE KIDS"**.

9 **MICK CARTER** ON **"EASTENDERS"**.

10 THREE-TIME HEAVYWEIGHT BOXING CHAMPION OF THE WORLD.

11 *DEF LEPPARD* GUITARIST.

12 LONG-TIME CAPTAIN ON *"NEVER MIND THE BUZZCOCKS"*.

13 GRIME MUSIC PIONEER, REAL NAME *DYLAN KWABENA MILLS*, HIS HITS INCLUDE *"DANCE WIV ME"*, *"BONKERS"*, *"HOLIDAY"* AND *"DIRTEE DISCO"*.

14 SINGER/SONGWRITER AND POLITICAL ACTIVIST, HIS ALBUM TITLES INCLUDE *"TALKING WITH THE TAXMAN ABOUT POETRY"*.

1001 ANSWERS

William Arthur Bonds MBE (pg 2)

1. Frank Lampard Sr.
2. Bobby Moore   3. Trevor Brooking
4. Alvin Martin   5. Jimmy Ruffell
6. Steve Potts   7. Vic Watson
8. Geoff Hurst

"The Moyesiah" (pg 4)

1. Lou Macari   2. Harry Redknapp
3. Glenn Roeder   4. Trevor Brooking
5. Alan Pardew   6. Alan Curbishley
7. Kevin Keen   8. Sam Allardyce
9. Slaven Bilić   10. Gianfranco Zola

"Mad Dog" Manny (pg 6)

1. Eintracht Frankfurt
2. Karlsruher SC
3. Bayer Leverkusen
4. Borussia Mönchengladbach
5. 1899 Hoffenheim
6. Karlsruher SC   7. FC Schalke 04
8. Hamburger SV

Moving On Up (pg 8)

1. Carlton Cole   2. David Cross
3. Frank McAvennie
4. Paulo Di Canio
5. François Van der Elst

The Boy Wonders (pg 10)

1. Reece Oxford   2. Neil Finn
3. Rio Ferdinand   4. Frank Lampard
5. Frank Nouble

Crescent Stars (pg 12)

1. Gökhan Töre
2. Sofiane Feghouli

3. Julien Faubert   4. Ricardo Vaz Tê
5. Demba Ba   6. Lucas Neill

The Boys of 1964 (pg 14)

1. Detroit Cougars
2. Torquay United
3. Charlton Athletic
4. Torquay United   5. Fulham
6. Leyton Orient   7. Crystal Palace
8. Stoke City
9. Sheffield Wednesday

The Geordie Lad (pg 16)

1. John Hartson
2. Robert Snodgrass
3. Enner Valencia   4. Dimitri Payet
5. Steve Lomas   6. Phil Parkes
7. Issa Diop   8. Felipe Anderson
9. Ray Stewart   10. Marc-Vivien Foé
11. David James   12. Luís Boa Morte
13. Pablo Fornals   14. Jarrod Bowen

The Africans (pg 18)

1. Senegal   2. Nigeria   3. Cameroon
4. Ivory Coast   5. DR Congo
6. Ghana   7. Algeria   8. Guinea
9. Mali   10. Equatorial Guinea

Harry's Florin Folly (pg 20)

1. Olympique Lyon
2. Derby County   3. Liverpool
4. Blackburn Rovers
5. Newcastle United
6. Sheffield Wednesday
7. Southampton   8. Benfica
9. Crystal Palace
10. Newcastle United   11. QPR
12. Ipswich Town   13. AC Milan
14. Nottingham Forest

The Goal Machine (pg 22)

1. Geoff Hurst   2. John Dick
3. Jimmy Ruffell   4. Tony Cottee
5. Johnny Byrne   6. Pop Robson
7. Trevor Brooking
8. Malcolm Musgrove
9. Martin Peters   10. David Cross

It's A Family Affair (pg 24)

1. Rio, Anton and Les Ferdinand
2. Alex and Rigobert Song
3. Iain and Natasha Dowie
4. Ian Wright and Shaun and Bradley Wright-Phillips
5. Ken and Kenny Brown
6. Steve and Daniel Potts
7. Lee   8. Allen

A Knight's Tale (pg 26)

1. Julian Dicks   2. Lawrie Leslie
3. Winston Reid
4. Sébastien Schemmel
5. Bobby Moore   6. Scott Parker
7. Danny Gabbidon

"Life Is So Good in America" (pg 28)

1. Clyde Best
2. Bobby Moore and Geoff Hurst
3. Jonathan Spector
4. Jim Standen   5. Ade Coker
6. Carlton Cole   7. Harry Redknapp
8. Ian Bishop   9. Alan Taylor

The Czech Stopper (pg 30)

1. Alex Král 2. Vladimír Coufal
3. Tomáš Souček   4. Radoslav Kováč
5. Marek Štěch 6. Jan Laštůvka
7. Pavel Srníček   8. Tomáš Řepka

Chapmania! (pg 32)

1. Stoke City   2. Malcolm Allison
3. Arsenal   4. Pop Robson
5. Sheffield Wednesday
6. Brian Clough
7. Howard Wilkinson
8. Billy Bonds   9. Ipswich Town
10. Swansea City

34 Years, Man and Boy … (pg 34)

1. Phil Parkes   2. Liam Brady
3. Ray Stewart   4. John Radford
5. David Cross   6. Julian Dicks
7. Tony Gale

He Could've Been a Contender (pg 36)

1. Norwich City
2. Lawrie McMenemy
3. Notts County   4. Manchester City
5. Leyton Orient   6. Torquay United
7. Wimbledon

The Boys of 1980 (pg 38)

1. Ipswich Town   2. St Johnstone
3. Southend United
4. Leyton Orient   5. Watford
6. Tottenham Hotspur
7. Manchester City   8. Manurewa
9. Crystal Palace

Hammers & Potters (pg 40)

1. Matthew Etherington
2. Luke Chadwick   3. Lawrie Leslie
4. Matthew Upson
5. Abdoulaye Faye
6. Marko Arnautović

"The Terminator" (pg 42)

1. Stewart Downing 2. Titi Camara
3. Yossi Benayoun 4. Adrián
5. Rigobert Song

Three Lions Irons (pg 44)

1. Frank Lampard 2. Rio Ferdinand
3. Stuart Pearce 4. Joe Hart
5. Martin Peters 6. Joe Cole
7. David James 8. Geoff Hurst
9. Trevor Brooking
10. Stewart Downing
11. Michael Carrick 12. Ian Wright
13. Matthew Upson 14. Scott Parker
15. Alvin Martin 16. Trevor Sinclair

The Wild Rover (pg 46)

1. Ian Pearce 2. Benni McCarthy
3. John Radford 4. Lars Jacobsen
5. Lucas Neill 6. Christian Dailly
7. Robbie Slater 8. Matty Holmes

Hey, Big Spenders! (pg 48)

1. Dale Gordon 2. Joey Beauchamp
3. Florin Răducioiu 4. John Hartson
5. Marc-Vivien Foé
6. Don Hutchison 7. Tomáš Řepka
8. Dean Ashton 9. Savio Nsereko
10. Matt Jarvis 11. Andy Carroll
12. André Ayew 13. Issa Diop
14. Felipe Anderson

Reggae Boyz Recruit (pg 50)

1. Trinidad and Tobago
2. Jamaica
3. Antigua & Barbuda
4. Saint Kitts and Nevis
5. Martinique
6. Trinidad and Tobago

7. Martinique 8. Martinique
9. Bermuda 10. Jamaica

The Golden Boys (pg 52)

1. Jimmy Greaves 2. Geoff Hurst
3. Ian Wright 4. Liam Brady
5. Martin Peters 6. Trevor Brooking
7. Teddy Sheringham
8. Stuart Pearce 9. Rio Ferdinand
10. Frank Lampard
11. Justin Fashanu

The Conveyor Belt (pg 54)

1. Lee Bowyer 2. Bobby Zamora
3. Alan Curbishley 4. Tony Carr
5. Paul Konchesky

Manuel's Men (pg 56)

1. Toulouse 2. Borussia Dortmund
3. Eintracht Frankfurt 4. Villarreal
5. Basel 6. Lazio 7. Arsenal
8. Corinthians 9. Fulham
10. Arsenal 11. Fiorentina
12. Espanyol 13. Millwall

The Name is Bond ... John Bond (pg 58)

1. Bobby Gould 2. Leroy Rosenior
3. Igor Štimac 4. Frank O'Farrell
5. Stuart Pearce 6. Paul Ince
7. Chris Hughton 8. Iain Dowie
9. Noel Cantwell 10. Ken Brown
11. Malcolm Allison 12. Martin Allen

Man U Men (pg 60)

1. Jesse Lingard 2. Carlos Tevez
3. Noel Cantwell 4. David Bellion
5. Jonathan Spector

6. Raimond van der Gouw
7. Roy Carroll   8. Stuart Pearson

Allez les Bleus! (pg 62)

1. Bernard Lama   2. Marc Keller
3. Alou Diarra   4. Morgan Amalfitano
5. Dimitri Payet   6. Patrice Evra
7. Kurt Zouma   8. Alphonse Areola

Go West, Young Man (pg 64)

1. Harry Redknapp   2. Carl Fletcher
3. Jack Collison   4. Matty Holmes
5. Jimmy Neighbour
6. Jimmy Quinn

The South Americans (pg 66)

1. Uruguay   2. Argentina
3. Paraguay   4. Chile   5. Peru
6. Ecuador   7. Brazil   8. Parguay
9. Colombia 10. Argentina
11. Colombia   12. Chile

Toffee Hammers! (pg 68)

1. Kurt Zouma   2. Don Hutchison
3. Lucas Neill   4. Tony Cottee
5. David Unsworth
6. Enner Valencia   7. Richard Wright
8. Nikola Vlašić   9. Slaven Bilić
10. Lars Jacobsen

Big Mal (pg 70)

1. Leroy Rosenior
2. Frank O'Farrell
3. Bobby Gould   4. Igor Štimac
5. Ron Greenwood
6. Bernard Lama   7. Harry Redknapp
8. Igor Štimac   9. Avram Grant
10. Noel Cantwell

11. Paulo Wanchope
12. Avram Grant

Managerial Merry-Go-Rounds (pg 72)

1. Avram Grant   2. Gianfranco Zola
3. Harry Redknapp   4. Glenn Roeder
5. Alan Pardew   6. Sam Allardyce
7. Slaven Bilić   8. David Moyes
9. Manuel Pellegrini

Last Line of Defense (pg 74)

1. England   2. Scotland   3. Canada
4. Czech Republic   5. Scotland
6. England   7. Northern Ireland
8. France   9. Trinidad and Tobago
10. Serbia   11. USA
12. Northern Ireland   13. England
14. Finland

Making an Entrance! (pg 76)

1. Ian Wright   2. Manuel Lanzini
3. Ken Tucker   4. Tony Cottee
5. Carlton Cole   6. Jesse Lingard
7. Freddie Sears

Curbs Your Enthusiasm (pg 78)

1. Birmingham City
2. Newcastle United
3. Liverpool
4. Newcastle United
5. Bordeaux
6. Fulham   7. Lazio
8. Tottenham Hotspur
9. Blackburn Rovers
10. West Bromwich Albion
11. Torino   12. Sevilla
13. Everton   14. Wigan Athletic
15. Newcastle United

Duty Calls (pg 80)

1. Ron Greenwood
2. Bobby Robson
3. Gareth Southgate
4. Glenn Hoddle 5. Fabio Capello
6. Walter Winterbottom
7. Alf Ramsey 8. Don Revie
9. Graham Taylor
10. Kevin Keegan 11. Roy Hodgson
12. Terry Venables
13. Ron Greenwood
14. Sven-Göran Eriksson
15. Alf Ramsey

Samba Soccer (pg 82)

1. Wellington Paulista
2. Felipe Anderson 3. Nenê
4. Javier Mascherano
5. Bernardo Rosa 6. Pablo Armero
7. Jonathan Calleri
8. Fabián Balbuena
9. Mauro Zárate 10. Ilan

Well, I Never ... (pg 84)

1. Tyrone Mears 2. Carlos Tevez
3. Tony Cottee 4. Victor Moses
5. Stephen Bywater
6. Rio Ferdinand
7. Slaven Bilić
8. Cockney Rejects
9. Ray Wilson
10. Bobby Ferguson

The Crystal Method (pg 86)

1. Iain Dowie 2. Hayden Mullins
3. James Tomkins
4. Johnny Byrne
5. Neil Ruddock
6. Paul Kitson

"He's Harder Than Jaap Stam ..." (pg 88)

1. Espanyol 2. Manuel Lanzini
3. Lionel Scaloni
4. Mauricio Taricco
5. San Lorenzo, River Plate
6. Jonathan Calleri
7. Manchester United
8. "The Little Chief"

The Ones That Got Away (pg 90)

1. Sol Campbell 2. John Terry
3. Kieran Richardson
4. Jimmy Bullard 5. Jlloyd Samuel
6. Freddy Eastwood 7. Fitz Hall

Hammer Rams! (pg 92)

1. Paulo Wanchope
2. Igor Štimac 3. Tyrone Mears
4. Stephen Bywater
5. Dave Swindlehurst 6. Rob Lee
7. Derek Hales 8. James Tomkins
9. Simon Webster

Irons Down Under (pg 94)

1. Martin Peters 2. Lucas Neill
3. Bobby Ferguson
4. Dylan Tombides
5. Stan Lazaridis 6. Hayden Foxe
7. Robbie Slater
8. Richard Garcia

His Name is Rio (pg 96)

1. Bobby Moore (1962, 1966, 1970), Peter Shilton (1982, 1986, 1990), Frank Lampard (2006, 2010, 2014)
2. David Seaman
3. Trevor Brooking

4. Bobby Moore   5. Rob Green
6. Stuart Pearce   7. Frank Lampard
Sr. and Frank Lampard   8. Sven-
Göran Eriksson, Fabio Capello,
Steve McClaren, Glenn Hoddle,
Kevin Keegan, Howard Wilkinson,
Peter Taylor

Getting Shirty! (pg 98)

1. Middlesbrough
2. Wolverhampton Wanderers
3. Internazionale   4. Liverpool
5. Swindon Town   6. West Ham
7. Wolverhampton Wanderers
8. Middlesbrough   9. Liverpool
10. Internazionale

¡Viva España! (pg 100)

1. Barcelona   2. Villarreal
3. Espanyol   4. Racing Santander
5. Real Betis   6. Sevilla
7. Deportivo La Coruña
8. Valencia   9. Real Madrid
10. Espanyol

The Early Bath (pg 102)

1. Pablo Zabaleta   2. Victor Moses
3. Michail Antonio   4. Lee Bowyer
5. John Hartson
6. Frédéric Piquionne
7. Jussi Albert Jääskeläinen
8. Tomáš Souček

Taking Early Retirement (pg 104)

1. Arsenal   2. FK Rostov
3. Blackburn Rovers   4. West Ham
5. Birmingham City
6. Blackburn Rovers

7. Tottenham Hotspur
8. Blackburn Rovers
9. Norwich City
10. Tottenham Hotspur

Old Glory! (pg 106)

1. Pavel Srníček   2. David James
3. Phil Parkes   4. Joe Hart
5. Adrián   6. Jussi Jääskeläinen
7. Mervyn Day   8. Jim Standen
9. Les Sealey   10. Roy Carroll
11. Robert Green
12. Manuel Almunia

Cottagers and Hammers (pg 108)

1. Leroy Rosenior
2. Paul Konchesky
3. Ray Houghton
4. Bobby Zamora   5. Brian Dear
6. Rufus Brevett   7. Tony Gale
8. Ryan Fredericks

His Name Was Zola ... (pg 110)

1. Brescia   2. AS Livorno
3. Spartak Moscow   4. Toulouse
5. Fiorentina   6. Blackburn Rovers
7. Grasshoppers   8. Internazionale
9. Villarreal   10. Saint-Étienne
11. Middlesbrough
12. Charlton Athletic

Czech Hammers (pg 112)

1. Tomáš Řepka
2. Luděk Mikloško   3. Alex Král
4. Radoslav Kováč
5. Pavel Srníček
6. Vladimír Coufal

Robbie Keane: Goal Machine (pg 114)

1. Aston Villa   2. Coventry City
3. Los Angeles Galaxy
4. Leeds United
5. Tottenham Hotspur
6. Internazionale   7. Celtic
8. Leeds United
9. Wolverhampton Wanderers
10. Liverpool

Big Sam's Gamble (pg 116)

1. Pachuca
2. Wolverhampton Wanderers
3. Anderlecht   4. Liverpool
5. Ipswich Town   6. Aston Villa
7. Milton Keynes Dons
8. Bolton Wanderers
9. Bristol City   10. Portsmouth
11. Barnsley   12. VfL Wolfsburg
13. Aston Villa
14. Bolton Wanderers
15. Stoke City   16. Sunderland
17. Arsenal   18. Chelsea
19. Liverpool   20. Barcelona

England Expects (pg 118)

1. Bobby Moore   2. Trevor Brooking
3. Stuart Pearson   4. Les Ferdinand
5. Rio Ferdinand   6. Trevor Sinclair
7. Paul Konchesky   8. Rob Green
9. Carlton Cole   10. Andy Carroll
11. Jesse Lingard
12. Aaron Cresswell   13. Declan Rice

Hoops! ... I Did It Again (pg 120)

1. John Hartson   2. Lou Macari
3. Frank McAvennie
4. David Moyes   5. Eyal Berkovic

The Champions (pg 122)

1. Manchester United
2. Liverpool   3. Real Madrid
4. Chelsea   5. Manchester United
6. Porto   7. Real Madrid

FWA Footballer of the Year (pg 124)

1. Clive Allen   2. Gianfranco Zola
3. Teddy Sheringham
4. Frank Lampard   5. Scott Parker

Hammer Hart (pg 126)

1. Nottingham Forest
2. Swansea City   3. Stoke City
4. Bayer Leverkusen   5. Marseille
6. Al-Jazira Club   7. Hull City
8. Juventus   9. Southampton
10. Olympiacos   11. Sion
12. Sampdoria   13. Leeds United
14. Maldonado   15. Hull City
16. Besiktas   17. Halmstads BK
18. Hamilton Academical
19. Fenerbahçe
20. Birmingham City
21. Borussia Mönchengladbach
22. Real Madrid   23. Valencia
24. Manchester City

Hammers on the Box (pg 128)

1. Wayne Bridge   2. David James
3. Ian Wright   4. Harry Redknapp
5. Jimmy Greaves   6. Neil Ruddock

French Imports (pg 130)

1. Paris Saint-Germain
2. Marseille   3. Lyon   4. Metz
5. Saint-Étienne
6. Paris Saint-Germain

7. Bordeaux   8. Toulouse
9. Paris Saint-Germain   10. Lyon

The Tenacious One (pg 132)

1. Liverpool   2. Newcastle United
3. Celtic   4. West Ham
5. Cardiff City   6. Manchester City
7. Norwich City   8. Coventry City

Marching On Together (pg 134)

1. Brian Deane   2. Sam Byram
3. Lee Bowyer   4. Matt Kilgallon
5. Rob Green   6. George McCartney
7. Robert Snodgrass
8. Hogan Ephraim   9. Lee Chapman
10. Robbie Keane

The Centurions (pg 136)

1. Javier Mascherano
2. Robbie Keane   3. Rigobert Song
4. Peter Shilton   5. Răzvan Raț
6. Niclas Alexandersson
7. Javier Hernández
8. Bobby Moore   9. Frank Lampard
10. Yossi Benayoun

Monikers (pg 138)

1. Alvin Martin   2. Neil Ruddock
3. Liam Brady   4. Ray Stewart
5. Johnny Byrne   6. John Bond
7. Geoff Hurst   8. Fitz Hall
9. Ronnie Boyce   10. Brian Dear
11. Fabián Balbuena
12. Carlos Tevez   13. Billy Bonds

Roeder's Recruits (pg 140)

1. Tomáš Řepka   2. Don Hutchison
3. Vladimír Labant   4. Kevin Horlock

5. David Connolly   6. Lee Bowyer
7. David Forde   8. David Noble
9. Raimond van der Gouw
10. Rufus Brevett
11. Neil Mellor
12. Matthew Kilgallon
13. Les Ferdinand
14. Gary Breen
15. Laurent Courtois
16. Matthew Etherington

The Middle Men (pg 142)

1. Martin Peters   2. Glen Johnson
3. Noel Cantwell   4. Rio Ferdinand
5. Kurt Zouma   6. Łukasz Fabiański
7. John Carew   8. Bobby Moore
9. Édouard Cissé   10. Kevin Nolan
11. Emmanuel Emenike
12. Ray Stewart   13. Nigel Reo-Coker
14. Tommy Yews   15. Jlloyd Samuel

Hello Goodbye! (pg 144)

1. Sam Allardyce   2. David Moyes
3. Lou Macari   4. Alan Pardew
5. Ron Greenwood
6. Gianfranco Zola   7. Slaven Bilić
8. Alan Curbishley
9. Manuel Pellegrini   10. Billy Bonds
11. Harry Redknapp   12. John Lyall

Pardew's Purchases (pg 146)

1. Norwich City   2. Racing Santander
3. Chelsea   4. Norwich City
5. Charlton Athletic   6. Cardiff City
7. Cardiff City   8. Sunderland
9. Preston North End
10. Hapoel Tel Aviv   11. Wimbledon

A Change of Heart (pg 148)

1. Martinique   2. Jamaica
3. Republic of Ireland   4. Senegal
5. Wales   6. Mali   7. Jamaica
8. Ghana   9. Northern Ireland
10. Trinidad and Tobago
11. Algeria   12. Republic of Ireland
13. Morocco   14. Northern Ireland

Poachers Turned Gamekeepers (pg 150)

1. Frank Lampard   2. Iain Dowie
3. Stuart Pearce   4. Harry Redknapp
5. Lee Bowyer   6. Ilie Dumitrescu
7. Malky Mackay   8. Chris Powell
9. Dave Sexton   10. Paulo
Wanchope   11. David Webb
12. Mervyn Day

Show Us Your Medals (pg 152)

1. Nottingham Forest 2. Chelsea
3. Birmingham City
4. Tottenham Hotspur
5. Oxford United
6. Nottingham Forest
7. Aston Villa   8. Liverpool
9. Manchester City
10. Tottenham Hotspur

Cape Crusaders! (pg 154)

1. Johnny Byrne   2. Luís Boa Morte
3. Geoff Hurst   4. John Sissons
5. Emmanuel Emenike
6. Bobby Moore   7. Perry Suckling

Teen Titans (pg 156)

1. Reece Oxford   2. Joe Cole
3. Chris Cohen   4. Alan Curbishley
5. Tony Cottee

Say What? (pg 158)

1. Paolo di Canio   2. Bobby Gould
3. Eyal Berkovic   4. Ray Houghton
5. Jimmy Greaves   6. Alf Ramsey
7. José Mourinho   8. Mark Noble

Armband of Brothers (pg 160)

1. Noel Cantwell
2. Phil Woosnam   3. Bobby Moore
4. Billy Bonds   5. Alvin Martin
6. Ian Bishop   7. Julian Dicks
8. Steve Potts   9. Steve Lomas
10. Paolo Di Canio
11. Christian Dailly
12. Nigel Reo-Coker
13. Lucas Neill   14. Matthew Upson
15. Kevin Nolan

Africa Cup of Nations (pg 162)

1. André Ayew
2. Frédéric Kanouté
3. Cheikhou Kouyaté
4. Rigobert Song
5. Benni McCarthy
6. Emmanuel Emenike
7. Victor Moses

Campeones (pg 164)

1. Alphonse Areola
2. Javier Mascherano
3. Paulo Futre   4. Benni McCarthy
5. Javier Hernández
6. Nikica Jelavić

National Heroes (pg 166)

1. Marko Arnautović
2. Tomáš Souček
3. Łukasz Fabiański
4. Frédéric Kanouté

5. Carlos Tevez
6. Freddie Ljungberg
7. John Carew
8. Javier Hernández
9. Paulo Futre   10. Robbie Keane

Where in the World? pg 168)
1. Malaysia   2. Thailand
3. Hong Kong   4. Indonesia
5. Djibouti   6. Iran   7. India
8. Singapore   9. New Zealand
10. Australia

Red Dragons (pg 170)
1. Demba Ba   2. Nikica Jelavić
3. Manuel Pellegrini
4. Slaven Bilić
5. Ricardo Vaz Tê
6. Marko Arnautović

Slaying Red Devils (pg 172)
1. John Dick   2. Martin Britt
3. Billy Jennings, Trevor Brooking
4. Ray Stewart, Geoff Pike
5. Frank McAvennie
6. Paolo Di Canio   7. Carlos Tevez
8. Manuel Lanzini

Ince To Inter (pg 174)
1. AC Milan   2. Juventus
3. Juventus   4. Tomáš Řepka
5. Pedro Obiang   6. Parma
7. Felipe Anderson   8. Lazio
9. Alessandro Diamanti
10. Valon Behrami

Greenwood the Great (pg 176)
1. Norwich City
2. Newcastle United
3. Sheffield Wednesday
4. Crystal Palace
5. Kilmarnock   6. Crystal Palace
7. Charlton Athletic   8. Chelsea
9. Tottenham Hotspur
10. Manchester United
11. Luton Town   12. Millwall
13. Sunderland   14. Airdrie United
15. Brighton & Hove Albion
16. Celtic   17. Hereford United
18. Sunderland

The Boys of 1994 (pg 178)
1. Florin Răducioiu   2. John Harkes
3. Rigobert Song, Marc-Vivien Foé
4. Ray Houghton, David Kelly

Any Old Irons (pg 180)
1. Jussi Jääskeläinen
2. Alvin Martin
3. Teddy Sheringham
4. Billy Bonds   5. Les Sealey
6. Stuart Pearce   7. Phil Parkes

Blue Men Group (pg 182)
1. Glen Johnson
2. Yossi Benayoun   3. Joe Payne
4. Victor Moses   5. Carlton Cole
6. Peter Brabrook

The Big Bosses (pg 184)
1:C 2:D 3:M 4:S 5:G 6:J
7:K 8:L 9:A 10:N 11:O 12:H
13:P 14:B 15:T 16:F 17:Q 18:I
19:R 20:E

Meet the New Boss, Same as the Old Boss (pg 186)

1. Sam Allardyce
2. Slaven Bilić
3. Gianfranco Zola
4. Harry Redknapp
5. Avram Grant
6. John Lyall
7. Sam Allardyce
8. Alan Pardew
9. Alan Curbishley
10. Glenn Roeder
11. David Moyes
12. Sam Allardyce
13. Avram Grant

Claret and Blue Dragons (pg 188)

1. Łukasz Fabiański
2. Ravel Morrison
3. Danny Gabbidon
4. Frank Nouble 5. Frank Lampard
6. Nicky Maynard 7. André Ayew
8. James Collins 9. Craig Bellamy

Avram's Additions (pg 190)

1. Pablo Barrera
2. Winston Reid
3. Gary O'Neil
4. Frédéric Piquionne
5. Wayne Bridge
6. Ruud Boffin
7. Thomas Hitzlsperger
8. Tal Ben Haim
9. Lars Christian Jacobsen
10. Victor Obinna

The Boys in Green (pg 192)

1. Gary Breen 2. Liam Brady
3. Darren Randolph
4. David Kelly 5. David Connolly

Goalgetter Glory (pg 194)

1. John Sissons, Geoff Hurst, Ronnie Boyce 2. Alan Sealey (2)
3. Johnny Byrne, Bobby Moore, Martin Peters 4. Alan Taylor (2)
5. Pat Holland, Keith Robson
6. Ray Stewart, Paul Goddard
7. Trevor Sinclair, Frank Lampard, Paolo Wanchope
8. Dean Ashton, Paul Konchesky, Jamie Carragher own goal

Bright Spark! (pg 196)

1. Sunderland, Queens Park Rangers
2. Chelsea, Liverpool, Aston Villa
3. Leeds United, Manchester United, Queens Park Rangers
4. Coventry City, Leeds United, Tottenham Hotspur, Liverpool, Aston Villa 5. Wigan Athletic, Chelsea, Liverpool, Stoke City
6. Queens Park Rangers, Nottingham Forest, Portsmouth, Southampton, West Bromwich Albion 7. Everton, Portsmouth, Sheffield United, Wigan Athletic
8. Wigan Athletic, Hull City
9. Chelsea, Charlton Athletic, Aston Villa 10. Norwich City, Queens Park Rangers
11. Bolton Wanderers, Chelsea, Manchester City, Sunderland, Portsmouth, Queens Park Rangers
12. Sheffield Wednesday, Charlton Athletic

Bad Boys, Bad Boys (pg 198)

1. Tomáš Řepka
2. Paolo Di Canio
3. James Tomkins
4. Frank McAvennie
5. John Hartson
6. Mark Ward
7. Ravel Morrison

German Imports (pg 200)

1. Borussia Dortmund
2. Eintracht Frankfurt
3. VfL Wolfsburg
4. Borussia Mönchengladbach
5. Karlsruher SC   6. 1899 Hoffenheim
7. FC Schalke 04
8. Hamburger SV
9. Karlsruher SC

Hammer Celebs (pg 202)

1. Ray Winstone
2. Steve Harris
3. Keira Knightley
4. James Corden
5. Kriss Akabusi
6. David Essex
7. Alfred Hitchcock
8. Pixie Lott
9. Danny Dyer
10. Lennox Lewis
11. Phil Collen
12. Phill Jupitus
13. Dizzee Rascal
14. Billy Bragg

TRIVQUIZ

FROM ABBA TO ZAPPA, AMÉLIE TO ZULU, AND AGÜERO TO ZIDANE

NEW FOOTBALL AND POP CULTURE QUIZZES EVERY DAY AT TRIVQUIZ.COM

trivquiz.com   trivquiz   trivquiz   trivquizcomic